P E R R Y
Inheriting Your Anc
Spirits, or l

RETURN OF THE
DARK
ANGEL

Expose the Sequence of Satanic Attacks
Against You and Your Family

RETURN OF THE DARK ANGEL

Published by Voice of Evangelism Ministries
P. O. Box 3595
Cleveland TN 37320
423.478.3456
www.perrystone.org

Unmarked Scripture quotations are from the King James Version of the Bible.

Scripture quotations marked NKJV are from the New Kings James Version of the Bible. Copyright © 1979, 1980, 1982 by Thomas Nelson, Inc., publishers. Used by permission.

First Edition © 2025

Printed in the United States of America

ISBN: 978-0-9895618-6-0

Cover Design/Illustration & Layout: Michael Dutton

CONTENTS

THE DARK ANGEL

The gentleman on the other end of the phone was someone who had never met me and who required an English interpreter to translate a revelation God had given Him. This minister has a global reputation for having an ear to hear from the Holy Spirit through the gift of the Word of Knowledge, and the words are astoundingly accurate.

On the phone, hundreds of miles away, he told me names of several people that I personally knew, all of whom he had no way of knowing. He revealed information so personal that only God Himself knew, including what I had prayed an hour earlier! Then he said to me, "*Every twelve years, Satan has assigned a dark angel to plot against you and your ministry.*"

After hearing this startling revelation, I spent days tracking this sequence, beginning with my birthday on June 23rd, 1959 and moving forward. I was surprised at what I had written on paper. In the span of sixty-five years, every twelve years, I had logged six types of unexpected or weird warfare incidents that I personally, the ministry, or my family had encountered. The biggest shock came when I discovered another cycle—a twelve-year *death cycle* on my mother's side of the family! I will share these discoveries in this book.

Unlocking this pattern caused me to think about thousands of our friends and ministry partners, and the possibility that they also might be unaware of their own patterns and cycles of spiritual warfare. How would your life be different if you could know far in advance the time when Satan will launch a strategized attack against you?

The enemy plans his attacks using people who, wittingly or unwittingly, fall under the spell of the evil one as they allow him to use them for his purposes. He can influence and manipulate people whose hearts and minds are not aligned with the heart and mind of God. It could be a friend, spouse, family member, coworker, church member, or someone you've never met.

What if you knew *in advance*, that the person you were planning to marry would eventually divorce you and leave you as a single parent to raise the children on your own? Would you continue with your plans to marry the person? Or, with the future being made known, would you pause and retreat from the engagement? What if you were warned of an impending accident when you make a trip? Would this motivate you to delay or cancel your plans?

God knows the enemy's plans, and He can and often does warn us of a coming trial, test, or spiritual assault. He reveals this to us through methods such as a vision, dream, scripture, inner burden, or a word of knowledge though the gifts of the Spirit (1 Cor. 12:7-10).

People who have survived great battles often become the instructors who teach others, by their own survival experience, how to maneuver through the darkest seasons. In this book I will disclose personal examples and lessons I have learned, along with scriptural insights and Hebrew and Greek word studies. Our reaction to physical, mental, and spiritual attacks must be founded on the battle principles taught throughout the Holy Bible, including unique verses and rules from heaven that some Christians might be unaware of.

You will also learn how to chart your own family patterns and cycles over time, including years in which the enemy is strategizing an attack or a counterattack. This is an important book for friends and partners of the ministry. It was birthed out of my own battles, as well as much sorrow over the deaths of family members.

CHAPTER 1

MY BESETTING SIN AND PERSONAL STRUGGLES

In my library is a book written in the 1950s by a noted healing evangelist. The title of the book is *My Besetting Sin*. I have in my private collection every book this man ever wrote. His emphasis in *My Besetting Sin* was Hebrews 12:1, which tells us to "lay aside the weight and the sin that does so easily beset us." The evangelist, rather than naming a specific sin, spoke of "the sin" as *any* sin that weighs a Christian down. He revealed the struggles that one might encounter in their walk with God.

Also in my library is an older booklet written by a noted evangelist titled, *That One Thing*. He never mentioned if he struggled with "one thing," but pointed out that many people fall short of their spiritual blessings because one thing—pride, unbelief, or some other sin—hinders their Christian walk.

Decades have gone by since these books were printed and passed through the hands of tens of thousands of readers. Yet, the subject material in both books remains an important message in our time.

The first minister *did* have a besetting sin. He could not sleep, and he occasionally drank alcohol, which was also a weakness in his family linage. While conducting a tent revival in Knoxville, Tennessee, he was arrested for driving intoxicated. He greatly loved the Lord and served Him in ministry. But a temptation was lurking nearby, ready to convince him that he needed a drink to help him sleep. He died in a hotel room after preaching in a large city, after seeing many salvations and miracles during decades ministry.

The second man also experienced a public moral failure. But after a season, he was restored to ministry after dealing with the "one thing" that hindered him.

Before questioning how two noted and anointed men of God could open a door that caused them such grief, look first in the mirror or check the skeletons in your own closet. The most outspoken critics often have their own past failures that they have hidden and locked away. Yet, these same people who take great pleasure in criticizing and exposing others never want their own sordid past exposed. Paul made an important observation when he said, "Some men's sins are open beforehand, going before to judgment; and some men they follow after" (1 Timothy 5:24). He was saying that some people's sins are exposed on earth, while other people's sins are not exposed until after they die and stand before God at judgment.

A BESETTING SIN

Scripture speaks of a sin that besets you. The Greek word for *beset* refers to something set up to thwart (trip up) an athlete in every direction. It is something that, if not dealt with, becomes a weight and burden in your spiritual race.

There are sins of the flesh and sins that defile your spirit. Some Christians are experts at categorizing sins and personally deciding which are acceptable or unacceptable. They sometimes debate a list of gray areas that the Bible doesn't specifically address. For example, God is clearly against lying. But was it acceptable to lie to protect the life of a Jewish neighbor hiding in your home during the holocaust? Some would call this a gray area.

Christians point out the eternal danger of yielding to biblically defined sins such as adultery, fornication, murder, idolatry, and so forth. Meanwhile, sins of the spirit, such as unforgiveness, bitterness, backbiting, strife and gossip, often are ignored. These transgressions are sins that corrupt and defile the spirit of a person (Heb. 12:15).

When I was growing up, it was common in traditional full-gospel congregations for church members to judge others by their outward appearance. The assumption was that, if you *looked* holy, if you wore no makeup or jewelry and wore only a certain type of clothing, then you must *be* holy. Some of the "holy" people who judged others harshly for outward appearance were unleashing sins of wrong attitudes and judgmentalism that defiled their own spirit and turned them into angry, pharisaical hypocrites.

Paul taught that a root of bitterness in your spirit will defile many (Heb. 12:15). The Greek word *defile* means "to spot or stain." The imagery is a clean, white garment being stained by dirt or wine. Someone whose mind and spirit are defiled, someone who has not dealt with their own root of bitterness, someone who uses negative and vicious words to assault people, will also taint and contaminate the thinking, emotions, and souls of others who listen to them. Before long, that one bitter person has successfully defiled the minds and spirits of those around them.

Do you find yourself dealing with a besetting sin?

TWO MEN'S BESETTING SINS

The Bible refers to the nature of the flesh as *carnal* (1 Cor. 3:3). The word carnal refers to the fleshly and sinful nature within a person. To be carnal is to focus on the abilities or frailties of the human nature

11

rather than the spiritual things of God. Allowing the carnal nature to rule can cause negative attitudes and wrong desires to foment. If carnality remains unchecked, any difficult season of trials and temptations will result in a seemingly sudden eruption of the carnal nature, much like magma builds under the earth's crust before a volcano erupts.

Both Samson and King David are two biblical examples of great deliverers who sometimes lacked discipline. Samson depended on his gift of supernatural strength to publicly display his great power. This frightened his enemies but impressed the beautiful Philistine women. Samson couldn't resist visiting Delilah's "hair salon" for a nap in her lap. He used his anointing from God to deliver *others,* but never applied it to *free himself* from a lustful desire for strange women. Note that the Spirit of God would come upon him, then lift from him, then return upon him, and then lift from him again (Judg. 13:25; 14:6, 19).

Some theologians will disagree when I say that the Spirit came upon him and then lifted from him. Samson never experienced the anointing that abided with him as believers do today, as indicated when John wrote, "The anointing abides in you..." (1 John 2:27). The abiding anointing was part of the new covenant blessing that was not available under the old covenant. Jesus taught His followers that the Spirit "dwells with you and shall be in you" (John 14:17). Samson was strong physically when the Spirit of God was upon him; but when the Spirit lifted, he was weak mentally.

David remained a faithful warrior and worshipper from his early teen years into his fifties, yet slowly he became a womanizer. At some point in mid-life, he took a flight from the fight. Instead of going to battle, he leaned on his mighty men of war who formed a militia to confront tribal enemies on his behalf. Alone at home without his personal male entourage, with his wife absent from the palace, David invited a beautiful woman to join him. He was a bored king who was avoiding the season when kings go to battle (2 Sam. 11:1). The woman,

Bathsheba, was married to a soldier named Uriah, who was more loyal to his job and his soldiers than he was interested in his wife. David's wife had mocked his worship. These were two people with obvious marital issues.

The same temptation of two lonely and needy people finding each other has replayed itself millions of times throughout history, as there is "nothing new under the sun" (Eccl. 1:9). David's affair began with a glance, a little romance, and a bit of prance, but it ended with a lance, as a sword struck David's house in judgment for David setting up the woman's husband, Uriah, to be killed in battle (2 Sam. 12:10).

Both Samson and David loved God, but both had a weakness for beautiful women; and not just one woman. Throughout the Bible are examples of people who loved the Lord but dealt with one or more sin or some carnal weakness. *The Bible also has examples of godly men such as Joshua, Daniel, and the prophets who seemingly never once failed or compromised.*

Christ taught to "watch and pray, lest you enter into temptation. The spirit is indeed willing, but the flesh is weak" (Matt. 26:41). The word for weak in Greek indicates something that is *infirm, feeble, or without strength.* The flesh, the carnal nature, has difficulty resisting whatever feeds it or makes it feel good. For example, when my wife tells our grandchildren that they can have ice cream after dinner, we suddenly watch them lose their appetite for healthy food. They are not hungry for dinner because all they can think about is the ice cream. They look at that green stalk of broccoli on their plate, and it doesn't compare to the thought of the delicious strawberry ice cream that will be dripping down their chins.

THE SOUL WARS

Peter revealed something important when he wrote, *"I beseech you as strangers and pilgrims, abstain from fleshly lusts, which war against the soul"* (1 Pet. 2:11 KJV). This war against the soul serves one of two purposes: to either destroy the soul through a lifestyle of sin, or to bring the soul into captivity like a prisoner being held at gunpoint.

In Hebrews 12:1 Paul spoke of spiritual weights and sins: *"...let us lay aside every weight, and the sin which so easily ensnares us, and let us run with endurance the race that is set before us...."* The Greek word *weight* refers to something that causes a burden or a hindrance in your body, soul, or spirit. An unclean habit or an addiction can be a weight.

Then there is *the* sin—a specific sin that we might call a "pet sin." Perhaps you want to do good, but evil is present (Rom. 7:21), and you are holding on to one thing that is slowing down your walk with God. The phrase *lay aside* refers to willingly laying down the hindrance and casting it away from you. Weights and pet sins create battles in your soul. If we continue to keep a door open, weights and sins will bring anxiety, anguish, and a burden.

A person's intellect, emotions, and senses are expressions of the human soul. A lifestyle of yielding to the carnal nature produces a war against the soul. When an unsaved person abides in unconfessed sins, eventually they may develop a seared conscience or a hardened heart, as they can act in a wicked manner without any remorse or repentance for their actions (1 Tim. 4:2). Followers of Christ who sin will immediately experience conviction; and if they do not repent, conviction should eventually pull them toward repentance.

As a longtime traveling evangelist, I often returned to the same churches for revivals year after year. I preached at one church for sixteen consecutive years, so I knew the congregation well. One man would show up every year, pray and repent at the altar, then gradually revert to his former lifestyle. This was a man who was dealing with a war in his soul. His battle was drug addiction, and he gained temporary relief through anointed church services that led to seasons of remorse. He was sorry for his actions, but the biblical word for *repent* means *to change your thoughts, attitudes, and behavior*. Repentance is the foundation of salvation and the Christian life.

MY OWN BATTLES

I once made a general list of things I had dealt with throughout nearly five decades of ministry. Some tests and trials lasted off and on for a few years.

As a teenager, I experienced rejection and bullying in school. In my early ministry, I dealt with visible demonic attacks at night, which continued for six months. For several years, off and on, I suffered with chronic depression. Before I was married, a group of drug dealers set out to hinder my ministry. Years later, after I learned about the successful conspiracy behind it, I wrote about it in a book called *Dealing with Hindering Spirits*. I was always interested in studying and preaching topics that nobody else was teaching at the time, which brought persecution from some denominational leaders who viewed the preaching of the Hebraic roots of Christianity as some form of heresy. This controversy caused rejection from some denominational leaders that persisted for two decades.

For nine years, my wife and I interceded and contended for our son's deliverance from alcohol and drug addiction. After non-stop ministry, when I turned fifty-five, I battled mental attacks, physical weariness, and insomnia. By age sixty, I was medically diagnosed with burnout and emotional exhaustion that included trauma. For three years, we dealt with public attacks, distortions, and numerous lies being spread about me, my family, and even some of my office staff. Today I still deal occasionally with medical issues that cause physical exhaustion.

Some things stretched on for years; others would surface for a season then disappear. After I wrote out a list, I wondered how I made it through so many years of hindrances, distractions, weariness, persecution, and criticism.

PAUL HAS THE ANSWER

It's easy to muse over all our own troubles until we read Paul the Apostle's ministry resume. Consider all the strange, negative, and dangerous circumstances he suffered:

> "Are they ministers of Christ? - I speak as a fool - I am more; in labors more abundant, in stripes above measure, in prisons more frequently, in deaths often. From the Jews five times received I forty stripes minus one. Three times I was beaten with rods, once was I stoned; three times I was shipwrecked; a night and a day I have been in the deep.

> "In journeys often, in perils of waters, in perils of robbers, in perils of my own countrymen, in perils of the Gentiles, in perils in the city, in perils in the wilderness, in perils in the sea, in perils among false brethren; in weariness and toil, in sleeplessness often, in hunger and thirst, in fasting often, in cold and nakedness - besides the other things, what comes upon me daily, my deep concern for all the churches."

> – 2 Corinthians 11:23-28 (NKJV)

God revealed to Paul the real secret to his survival: *"My grace is sufficient for you, and my strength is made perfect in weakness"* (2 Cor. 12:9). God gives each of us grace and favor that we cannot earn by human merit.

Consider God's grace and favor working in Paul. When Paul was under a death threat in Damascus, he escaped by being lowered in a basket (Acts 9). He was jailed with Silas, beaten, and confined in wooden stocks. God sent an earthquake that liberated both preachers, along with the entire prison population (Acts 16). Paul was stoned in Lystra and left lying on the ground as dead. After the disciples' prayed, he suddenly arose and journeyed the following day to a new destination. This was a true miracle, because when people were stoned, they were stoned until dead (Acts 14).

Paul survived a shipwreck and potential drowning by floating on a plank from the broken ship (Acts 27). After the wreck, while collecting firewood he was bitten by a deadly viper; yet the poison had no effect (Acts 28). God protected Paul in every dangerous and deadly situation and kept him alive until he completed his assignments. No weapon formed against him could prosper (Isa. 54:17). How I have survived and how you survive is the same way that Paul survived; it is through the grace and favor of God!

When we know a battle is coming, we can often prepare in advance. The battles that hit without warning require time, patience, and trust in God. "Weeping may endure for a night, but joy comes in the morning" (Psalm 30:5). We are built to withstand storms, remain standing through tests, and outlast trials. As David wrote, *"I would have lost heart, unless I had believed that I would see the goodness of the Lord in the land of the living"* (Psalm 27:13).

We will make it through if we follow His Word and wait to experience the goodness of the Lord. Ask God for His help and follow the instructions provided in Scripture. Lay aside every weight and any besetting sin, and walk in spiritual freedom. This is the will of God for you.

CHAPTER 2

SATAN HAS A TARGET ON YOUR FIRSTBORN CHILD

In many families, out of all the children, their firstborn is the one who struggles the most spiritually, mentally, or emotionally. I began to understand this battle over a firstborn after our son Jonathan was born.

In the late 1980s, I had a dream and saw two young children, both girls, playing on a backyard swing set. One stood out, as she was slightly prissy and full of personality. When I asked her who she was, she replied, "I'm Amanda. I'm the girl you're going to have." When Pam found that she was expecting, we both *assumed* it would be one of the little girls I saw in the dream. Pam's friends bought frilly dresses and we painted the baby's room pink because we thought a girl was coming.

However, it was not time for Amanda to enter the world. Two incidents occurred long before we discovered that our firstborn would be a boy. While ministering in Florida, a man who spent much time in prayer announced to Pam and me that our first child would be a son. At the time, we didn't plan to have a child since we traveled so much, sometimes being away from home for sixteen weeks straight. When Pam announced she had conceived, a dear ministry partner wrote us a letter that said, "You will have a son before you have a daughter," and quoted Scripture that speaks about the firstborn male being holy to the Lord.

At that time, I had been in full time traveling ministry about twelve years and thought I knew the scriptures quite well. However, the passage about the male firstborn child being set apart by the Lord never registered with me. My friend had penned the verses from the Bible which read:

> "Then the LORD spoke to Moses, saying, "Consecrate to Me all the firstborn, whatever opens the womb among the children of Israel, both of man and beast; it is Mine."
>
> — EXODUS 13:1-2 (NKJV)

> "Everything that first opens the womb of all flesh, which they bring to the LORD, whether man or beast, shall be yours; nevertheless, the firstborn of man you shall surely redeem, and the firstborn of unclean animals you shall redeem. And those redeemed of the devoted things you shall redeem when one month old, according to your valuation, for five shekels of silver, according to the shekel of the sanctuary, which is twenty gerahs."
>
> — NUMBERS 18:15-17 (NKJV)

These verses also serve as a foundation for the spiritual "law of the first." The first (first fruits) always belongs to the Lord, as this represents the seed for all future blessings. During the festival of first fruits, the first ripened grains or fruits were presented as holy to the Lord (Exod. 34:26). The first of tithe also belongs to the Lord.

At 5:30 in the morning on December 23, 1989, our precious firstborn child, a son that we named Jonathan Gabriel, arrived on the coldest morning in the history of Cleveland, Tennessee. He was born four weeks early and remained in the hospital four extra days with jaundice. We brought him home two days after Christmas weighing 5 pounds and 4 ounces. He was so tiny they slipped him into a red

Christmas stocking and handed him to Pam. To us he was the best gift we had ever received.

EARLY ONE HALLOWEEN MORNING

Within a month, Jonathan was on the road with us, as my ministry schedule was full in 1990. Sometimes he flew on planes, while other times he slept in a baby carrier in the back seat of our van.

That year the little fellow started waking up at 12:30 every night and crying the most pitiful cry. We would jump up and go to the crib, pick him up, and try to console him. At first we assumed he was hungry, but many times he didn't respond to feeding, either. This went on for months without any explanation.

One night when Jonathan was ten months old, something bizarre happened. He was lying between Pam and me in our bed when suddenly we heard him choking. I jumped up and turned on the light. He had vomited an orange substance, and we immediately picked him up. That was when I noticed something that appeared to be blood on both sides of his temples. It was no small amount of blood, and there was the appearance of a thumbprint, as if someone had dipped their thumbs in blood and smeared it on Jonathan's temples.

We were perplexed. We examined his fingers to see if he had scratched himself, but we found nothing. We searched the sheets and pillowcases but found no source of the blood. We checked ourselves and came up without a clue for why this blood had appeared on Jonathan's temples.

This happened on halloween night. Older people might remember growing up as children, dressing in a simple costume and hitting the neighbors up for candy. However, after exploring the origin of Halloween, our family has not participated in the event. I knew there was something suspicious about the blood on my son's temples, but I didn't immediately relate it to this occult holiday. I do recognize that the temples are close to the brain, and both hemispheres of the brain must function properly for a person to learn, reason, have normal emotions, and simply live life.

When I began to share this with close friends, I learned of two strange incidents that occurred in or near our hometown on that halloween night. A local newspaper reported that the head of a satanic organization based in San Francisco had been meeting with followers in Chattanooga, which is about thirty miles from Cleveland. The leader said he was sensing vibrations he did not like, and his visit was designed to interrupt and hinder the Christian progress in the region.

I learned of a second incident when a young man informed me about a dog that was found in their neighborhood after halloween, and it appeared to have the blood drained from it. With this strange combination, I began to suspect that some type of spirit had placed those blood marks on our son. Just the thought sent me into a spiritual rage! Such foes are never welcome in our house or on our property. My wife and I also did an internal house investigation to make sure there were no toys or objects that could be attracting negative forces. To be on the safe side, we removed a few things. Eventually the crying stopped, and Jonathan was able to rest.

THE BATTLE FOR THE FIRSTBORN

Growing up, Jonathan was energetic. At times I regretted how we had to carry him around from place to place, hardly ever being home and always eating out while on the road. He was a trooper. However, when he entered his teens, a new battle emerged in his life. I remembered the attack on him as an infant, and realized this one-time incident may have been part of a larger strategy to impact him and disrupt his destiny. He entered a firstborn battle that lasted at least nine years.

I am sharing this to say that there is often a battle for your firstborn child. In churches I have asked, "How many of you have a firstborn child who is struggling more than your other children?" Sometimes as many as three-fourths of the people raise their hands. Often, their child is in bondage to an addiction that hinders them or causes problems in their marriage. Some have chosen alternative lifestyles. Battles begin with the enemy striking their mind with fiery darts when they are young (Eph. 6:16).

In the Stone family, my mother gave birth to four children, two boys and two girls. My older sister is the firstborn child, and I am the firstborn son. Both of us had our own distinct attacks when we were children. When my sister was about four years old, a doctor treated her for strep throat with an overdose of penicillin, which she was allergic to, then sulfa, which she also was allergic to. From there she developed scarlet fever and was hospitalized. Each day the doctors told our parents that she wouldn't make it through the night. Only prayer brought her through. Today she works as my personal assistant in the ministry.

When I was about two to three years of age, Dad was driving to Elkins, West Virginia with Mom and me in the front seat. I had been standing up on the seat between the two of them when Dad made me sit down. Soon after, he rounded a curve on a two-lane road and slammed into a vehicle that had stopped in his lane. There was no way he could hit the brakes in time, nor could he veer left due to oncoming traffic. His only choice was to brace himself and crash into the back of the vehicle in front of us.

Cars did not have seatbelts in those days, and my parents suffered some bad injuries from hitting the windshield, the steering wheel, and the dashboard. I was thrown against the dashboard and fell to the floor. By God's mercy, I was not seriously harmed and was taken to a church member's house while mom and dad were admitted to the hospital.

FIRSTBORN SONS IN THE BIBLE

According to the Torah, God required that the firstborn son be specially dedicated to God, as both man and beast belonged to Him. The firstborn son was also assigned privileges and responsibilities that the others did not have. The firstborn's birthright included a double portion of the estate and the assignment of head of household after his father's death. The firstborn was to care for his mother until her death.

God called Israel His firstborn son (Exodus 4:22), referring to His chosen firstborn nation with whom He had a covenant. Christ is the firstborn of the Father, and when He came into the world, all of God's angels worshipped Him (Heb. 1:6).

Scripture reveals the battles among numerous firstborn sons. The first wicked firstborn son mentioned in scripture was Er, the oldest son of Judah and the grandson of Jacob. Er was so wicked that God killed him (Gen. 38:6-7).

Isaac's firstborn son Esau sold his birthright to his brother Jacob in a time of hunger and weariness. Jacob took his brother's blessing by deceiving his father Isaac, who thought he was dying (Gen. 25:29-34 and 27:36). Thus, the biological firstborn, Esau, lot his birthright and his blessing.

Reuben was Jacob's firstborn. He slept with his father's concubine, resulting in Reuben losing his firstborn blessing. Jacob said that Reuben was "unstable as water and would not excel" (Gen. 49:4).

Another example was Nadab, the firstborn son of Aaron, Israel's first high priest. Aaron's sons Nadab and Abihu, both of whom were ordained to serve as priests, profaned an offering unto the Lord and died as a result (Num. 3:2-4).

JUDGMENT ON THE FIRSTBORN

The Egyptian Pharaoh mistreated the Hebrew people, enslaving them for generations and using their free slave labor to build treasure cities for the Egyptians (Exod. 1:11). When the time came for the Hebrews to return to the Promised Land, Pharaoh resisted releasing his free labor force, knowing that without the brickmakers and construction workers, his ego-stroking projects would sit unfinished in the sand.

The tenth plague that God sent to Egypt brought the death of all firstborn sons and animals. God protected the Hebrews' firstborn sons and animals by telling them to apply lamb's blood on the sides and upper doorposts. When the destroying angel saw the lamb's blood, he was forced to "pass over" those homes, and no plague would befall them. Thus, the celebration of Passover was initiated (see Exodus 12).

God's original intent for Israel was that all firstborn males be separated to Him for the purpose of future tabernacle and temple ministry. However, the Lord later appointed the tribe of Levi to be His first chosen as ministers:

> *"Then the LORD spoke to Moses, saying: 'Now behold, I Myself have taken the Levites from among the children of Israel instead of every firstborn who opens the womb among the children of Israel. Therefore, the Levites shall be Mine, because all the firstborn are Mine. On the day that I struck all the firstborn in the land of Egypt, I sanctified to Myself all the firstborn in Israel, both man and beast. They shall be Mine: I am the LORD.'"*

> — NUMBERS 3:11-13 (NKJV)

Throughout the Bible, the firstborn, especially a son, was the leader among the siblings and was the closest to his father. At death, the firstborn was to step in and oversee the family. An attack on the firstborn was a disruption in God's flow for the family.

GOOD PARENTS — BAD CHILDREN

A puzzling aspect of raising children is how bad parents can end up with children serving the Lord, or how godly parents might see their children stray from faith and become rebellious toward spiritual truth. This is part of what Paul termed *the mystery of iniquity* (lawlessness) in 2 Thessalonians 2:7.

Samuel was the prophet who rejected Saul as king and anointed David in Saul's place. The older high priest Eli took Samuel under his covering, raised him in the Tabernacle of Moses, and ordained him to be Israel's future prophet. As a young child, Samuel heard God's voice (1 Sam. 3).

In Samuel's later years, he was blessed with a firstborn son named Joel and a second son named Abijah. In Samuel's day both sons were appointed judges. Yet his sons did not walk in his ways; they turned aside after dishonest gain, took bribes, and perverted justice. The tribes of Israel saw the political corruption and demanded that Samuel anoint a king over them, instead of his evil sons (1 Sam. 8:3-5).

Samuel became a strong, spiritual leader. He was a miracle child whom his barren mother Hannah had prayed to conceive. Hannah dedicated him back to the Lord to be raised as a prophet in Israel (1 Sam. 1-2). Yet his sons were corrupt.

In a similar fashion, how many mothers in the church have dedicated their infants to the Lord, only to watch them grow up, turn from their faith, and set out on their own journey of unrighteousness, breaking the heart of a praying mother and dad.

THE FIRSTBORN DAUGHTER'S BATTLE

Firstborn daughters can also be targeted. Lot escaped the destruction of the four cities with two unmarried daughters. The Jewish historian

Josephus writes that God gave a direct prophecy to Adam that the earth would be destroyed once by water and the second time by fire. Noah's flood occurred 1,556 years after Adam, and it destroyed the world's population, except for eight souls who were hidden safely in the ark (1 Pet. 3:20).

Some Jewish rabbis believe that when the fire destroyed the four large cities south of the Dead Sea, Lot's daughters thought everyone had been killed except for them. They say this because of a recorded statement that the firstborn daughter said to the younger daughter, "Our father is old, and there is not a man in the earth to come into us after the manner of all the earth" (Gen. 19:31). The firstborn daughter may have based her wrong assumption on the fact that fire destroyed the cities. She could have been thinking that this was the fulfillment of the ancient prophecy given to Adam, that the earth would be destroyed by fire.

The firstborn daughter influenced her younger sister to get their dad intoxicated. Both were impregnated by their father, who apparently was so inebriated that he was unaware of what had occurred. Lot fathered two sons.

Two conclusions can be drawn from this story. First, it is possible to *misinterpret what is happening around you.* God spared a small town of Zoar, and angels instructed Lot and his daughters to go there. However, they went up out of Zoar (Gen. 19:30) and lived in a cave in the mountains, thereby avoiding the town that was spared. They lived isolated, perhaps out of fear.

The danger of isolation is that it breeds loneliness, and when a person is lonely, the adversary easily plays mind games. Christ was completely alone, fasting for forty days in the wilderness of the Judean desert. He was temped of the devil during the forty days, as Mark noted, "He was in the wilderness forty days, being tempted of Satan" (Mark 1:13). Lot's daughter perceived that there were no men left with whom to have children, and therefore it was their responsibility to repopulate the region, just as Noah's three sons and their wives had done after the flood.

The second observation is the *influence* that the older daughter (firstborn) had over the younger. When the firstborn made the suggestion, the younger did not resist. Younger siblings often follow the patterns and actions of the older. If the firstborn son or daughter is strong in faith, the younger often will follow. If the firstborn is in bondage, sometimes the younger will follow the same path.

WHAT CAN PARENTS DO?

There are three observations from Scripture that parents of a spiritually straying child should understand and claim for their prodigal. I am aware that single mothers are often the spiritual leaders of the family, so this advice applies regardless.

First, we must train our children in the truth and plant seeds of Scripture from the earliest age (see Prov. 22:6). The child will often follow the mother during his or her early development, simply because of the emotional attachment to her. Then, if they stray, begin recalling both to God and to the child the seed that you planted in their heart as they were growing. God's Word is a seed that is incorruptible, and the seed of the life of God remains, even though the Word is not being obeyed.

My wife Pam has been an excellent example of a woman of God for our children and grandchildren. Our three grandchildren live next door and each day they come to Nana's house to hang out, play, and eat. They are taught to pray and give thanks. They love going to church. The oldest takes a plastic microphone and sings and dances around the room, while her younger siblings watch and imitate her. We encourage them to sing and pray.

The first principle is to set the example, especially while they're young. If you don't attend church, or if you criticize churches and ministers, then don't expect them to have the desire for God's house. You, as a parent (or guardian), are the seed planter. Never depend exclusively upon a local church alone to plant the seed, because planting the Word should happen first at home. People complain about no prayer in public schools, but the same parents who complain might never pray at home.

The second principle is to obey this verse: *"Train up a child in the way he should go, and when he is old, he will not depart from it"* (Prov. 22:6). *Train* can mean to give instruction, to develop, and to discipline. *The way they should go* refers to the path of righteousness and truth, and to lead them in the right direction. The Amplified version of the Bible expounds on this with, "teaching them to seek God's wisdom and will for their talents and abilities."

Training in the way they should go can also refer to observing the child's interests and helping to develop those interests. My oldest grandchild loves to sing, loves music, and says she is going to be a worship leader. We are already directing her along that path. The middle one loves art. She likes to sit with an art set and draw, which is what my daughter Amanda does. Today Amanda teaches art in a ministry school. We encourage the middle one to draw and paint pictures, as we are leading her in a place that is already in her heart. Find their interest and participate in leading them in the path of righteousness and the path of their destiny.

The third principle is to continually *hedge them in* through the power of prayer. When Job was surrounded by a hedge, Satan was unable to touch any part of Job's life (Job 1:10). It is possible that Job's hedge was an encampment of angels that kept the enemies of Job from accessing his home, family, animals and health, as "the angel of the Lord encamps around about those who fear the Lord" (Psa. 34:7).

My father, who spent his life in ministry, prayed every day and always spoke prayers over his children and grandchildren, calling them by name. I heard him petition God to let no harm, danger, or disabling accidents come to any family member. We have survived near accidents, close calls, sickness, and other forms of distress, as Dad's prayers are like seeds planted as a memorial in heaven.

I often bless my grandchildren by laying hands on their heads and sincerely praying for their protection and for God's will to be done in their lives.

THE LORD CAME THROUGH

The firstborn child of my friend Jentezen Franklin is his daughter Courtney. Courtney and Jonathan, my firstborn, were both in the same college together at the same time. Both were engaged in different battles where the enemy attempted to take them out through death. It took intense prayer and claiming God's family salvation promises, and today both are overcomers.

In April of 2024, Courtney stood before three thousand young people during Warrior-Fest at the Omega Center International where she ministered and gave her testimony. In the back of the room, operating some of the media equipment, was my son Jonathan. It was an emotional moment for me to see God's outcome in their lives.

When you have done all you can do to raise your children in the righteousness of the Lord and lead them along the right path, you must continue to pray for them without ceasing. Place your child and all your bloodline in the hands of the Lord. Claim this generational blessing of family salvation, *"Believe on the Lord Jesus Christ, and you shall be saved and your house"* (Acts 16:31). Also, pray that God will separate them from the wrong people and bring into their life a righteous person whom they like and respect, and pray that this person will be a positive influence.

We prayed for my son to find a wife who would understand his personality and complexities. God sent us a great daughter-in-law who was a perfect match for Jonathan, and they now have three young children. God won the firstborn battle.

CHAPTER 3

AN ANCESTOR'S SIN CAUSED THE DEATH OF TWO CHILDREN

Growing up I heard about a certain family photo, but I never saw it until decades later in November 2023 in Parsons, West Virginia. My two cousins and I were rummaging through my beloved Aunt Millie's belongings, who had passed away seven years earlier. Among stacks of papers on her bedroom dresser was a large manila envelope. Inside was the photo I had heard about but had never seen. Knowing the story behind it, I was overcome with sadness.

The black and white photo captured an unforgettable and heartbreaking moment in time—an image of two somber adults looking down at their five-year-old son in an open coffin. It told a story that my mother's family knew, but few people ever wanted to talk about.

My mother's grandfather, Pete Bava, immigrated from Italy in 1910 and settled in Pierce, West Virginia. Over time, he and my great-grandmother had four sons and three daughters—John, Joe, Tony, Daniel, Millie, Sarah, and Caroline. Sarah was Millie's twin who died shortly after birth. In the late 1920s, none of the family were serving the Lord.

The story as recalled by family members told of a place in Pierce, West Virginia called "the rock," where Pete and his drinking buddies made and stored moonshine. The Italian group met there to get intoxicated, and at times small children were present as well. On one occasion, eight-year-old John (who would one day become my maternal grandfather), handed a jar of moonshine to his five-year-old brother, Tony. He drank some of it, which led to his death from alcohol poisoning. I found a copy of Tony's death certificate, dated July 4, 1921, stating that his death was caused by fits and spasms.

My Granddad John would occasionally mention Tony and his death at a young age. But I never knew until many years later that it was John himself, an unsaved young boy, who handed Tony the moonshine on that fateful day.

Another son, Daniel, was born to Pete and his wife Lectie in 1914. According to family, it was a cold day in the mountains of West Virginia when all the men (and a few women) gathered at the rock to drink moonshine. Daniel, a one-year-old infant, was wrapped in a blanket, which blew off in the wind. The people were so absorbed with drinking moonshine that they didn't notice. Daniel became sick with double pneumonia and died.

At Rose Cemetery just outside the town of Thomas, West Virginia are the graves of my great-grandparents Pete and Lectie, my grandparents John and Lucy Bava, and three children I never had the chance to meet, Tony, Daniel, and Sarah. A tombstone of these little children is the silent reminder of the consequences of bad choices in one family.

The black and white photo captured a sad funeral scene as a reminder for future generations. Two little boys, uncles that I would not have a chance to know, had their lives cut short in an Italian family that, at the time, had no covenant relationship with Christ.

BREAKING THE SIN CYCLE

The good news is that, within the next decade, the entire family came to know the Lord. My Grandad Bava became a Gospel singer, songwriter, music publisher, and minister, in addition to working in the coal mines. Uncle Joe raised his ten children in the knowledge of the Lord. Aunt Millie and Aunt Caroline, both of whom are in heaven now, were strong in faith and were loyal followers of Christ. Both were partners of our ministry, and Millie rarely missed a conference.

I thought about what kind of life Tony and Daniel might have had. Would they have been ministers, too? How many children would they have raised? *Alcohol cost them their lives.* It was a family sin and weakness that was eventually dealt with, but it carried long-term sorrowful memories. This is why the converted children of Pete hated liquor so much. They saw what it cost them. Alcoholic beverages are sometimes referred to as "spirits." In my opinion, alcoholic beverages certainly open doors in people's lives for the *wrong type* of spirits.

THE STONE FAMILY LINEAGE

In the 1950s when the West Virginia coal mines were booming, the area around War and Welch, West Virginia was tagged, "West Virginia's Billion Dollar Coal Fields." The population in McDowell County, West Virginia was almost a hundred thousand people, with most of the men employed in the coal mines. By 2023, the county population had dropped to under eighteen thousand. Today the same towns have empty streets lined with old, abandoned, boarded up buildings, and it is considered an epicenter of economic depression.

My father, Fred Stone, was one of ten living brothers and sisters, all but two of whom have now passed away. As a teenager, he was invited to a revival by his older half-brother Morgan, who had a different father who died in a hunting accident. Before his conversion, Dad and Morgan fought to the point that, on one occasion, Dad fired a rifle a few inches above Morgan's head. Years later Dad confessed, "My intent was to kill Morgan. When I aimed for Morgan's head, a voice said to me, "Fred, if you pull that trigger and shoot your brother, your life is ruined forever. Don't do that." He wept as he continued, "At the last second, I jerked the rifle up and missed Morgan by a few inches. A few weeks later, in 1949, Morgan was converted to the Lord and was the person who invited me to the local revival, where I received Christ and turned my life around."

Dad lamented, "Not only would I have taken an innocent life, but I also would have taken the life of the man who would eventually lead me to Christ. I would have been in prison, never met your mother, and you (speaking to me) never would have been born. The entire destiny of the family would have been destroyed, all because of *one wrong decision*."

Dad reminded me of his teenaged cousin who died in prison after shooting and killing a classmate who bullied him. Another cousin shot a man in anger and spent most of his life in prison until he was released after many years. Each time Dad passed through White Sulphur Springs, West Virginia, he never missed an opportunity to stop and visit his cousin Darrie. When Dad told the story of his conflict with Morgan, I knew *why* he wanted to see Darrie. Dad felt pity for this man, as he could have found himself in the same situation, had he not followed that small voice in his head saying, "Don't do it!"

It was obedience to the conviction of the Holy Spirit and entering a redemptive covenant through Christ that changed the entire destiny of the Bava and Stone families. Fred Stone eventually met and married Juanita Bava, and they were blessed with two sons and two daughters. Today their lineage has seven grandchildren and three great-grandchildren, most of whom are following their footsteps in faith.

EMOTIONALLY CHARGED REACTIONS

Dad's story reveals the danger of *uncontrolled emotions* that fuel anger and rage and can motivate us to make either right or wrong decisions. In our culture today, the display of irrational emotions causes serious societal problems. People become offended and enraged at innocent and ordinary incidents they should simply brush off.

Irrational emotions can be deadly when they overtake the rational mind. Road rage is an example. I was driving behind my wife from Cleveland to Chattanooga when a woman cut her off, and then shot Pam a middle finger. Irrational emotions kicked in, and I jerked my SUV into the other lane and laid on the horn as I followed the woman. She sped up and I sped up. She switched lanes and I switched lanes. I must have followed her for two miles. Suddenly it hit me: I was reacting in the flesh. What good does this do? I repented and stopped the emotional reaction. Pam never even noticed what the woman did.

People are presently in prison because of an angry, emotional overreaction to a situation. Guns have been drawn and even small children have been shot dead. Was the irrational reaction to being triggered worth it? One gun, one bullet, and one minute of undisciplined emotions where someone shoots first and thinks later can cost one person their life and another person their lifetime of freedom.

THE EAR CHOPPING DISCIPLE

Peter was no doubt sincere when he promised Christ that he would never deny Him and would even be willing to go to prison and die with Him (Luke 22:33). To prove his promise, when six hundred Roman soldiers (a band - John 18:3) marched into the Garden of Gethsemane, Peter stood between the armed troops and Christ. He drew his sword and sliced off the ear of Malchus, a servant of Caiaphas, the high priest at the temple (John 18:10). Peter's reactions were often emotionally charged, and this bold assault proved he reacted without considering the possible consequences.

Once Peter's emotions calmed down and his reasoning kicked in gear, he realized that he could be charged with assault and sentenced to prison. As a Jew, he possibly could have been executed since the priesthood at that time was supervised by Rome's governmental authority.

Later, during Christ's trial, Peter denied three times that he knew Jesus, thereby placing a curse (anathema) upon himself to impress upon those sitting with him at the fire that he was not associated with Christ.

As ministers we often emphasize that Peter denied the Lord, then pick up the narrative after the resurrection when Christ restored Peter by asking him three times, "Do you love me?" Peter answered affirmatively, and Christ gave Peter a new commission to feed His sheep (John 21). We seldom emphasize the spiritual and emotional impact upon Peter when he lied and claimed not to know Jesus. When the rooster crowed a second time, Peter was reminded of his failure, and he broke down and wept.

In Mark 14:71, the word *cursed* does not mean Peter used profanity; it is the Greek word *anathema*. It is a strong Aramaic word meaning "to place upon a person a self-curse." At that moment, Peter bound himself with a great curse that spiritually expelled him from the house of Israel and from the synagogue. In the Greek language he essentially said, "If I know this man, let me be anathema—banished from God's presence!" Peter not only lied and denied, but he now was a cursed man. He was too fearful to appear at the cross, and instead he went into hiding. When Christ arose, He told Mary, "Go tell my disciples and Peter..." (Mark 16:7).

In Luke 22, Jesus had been in prayer and knew that Satan was coming to sift Peter. He revealed that Peter would fail the test. Christ also predicted that Peter would return and be converted, meaning that he would return to his original faith in Christ. This story reveals several facts about your own situations.

First, the Lord sees in advance every plot the enemy has set against us, long before it is launched. Second, He already knows if we will stand firm or fall when the attack comes. God is not taken by surprise when one of His children fails. He made a provision of return so that, if we sin, we have an advocate with the Father. When we confess, He is faithful and just to forgive us our sins and to cleanse us from all unrighteousness (1 John 1:9). Third, His desire is that we return to faith and help others in their times of difficulty and weakness.

BITTER PEOPLE, BITTER CHILDREN

Entire families are destroyed or divided due to the sin of bitterness. Several years ago, I met a director of a health facility that assists the elderly in their last stage of life. I asked her to tell me one of the most unusual things she had ever seen while working there. She told about an elderly woman who was the angriest and most difficult person she had ever met. Her children had her placed there with these instructions: We will pay the bill each month, but we never want to be contacted, for any reason, no matter what. When she dies, send her body to be cremated and we will pay the bill.

The director thought that was a harsh request until she had to deal with the woman. She had the foulest mouth the director had ever heard. She took God's name in vain, wanted no help from anyone, and explosively cursed at those who tried to assist her. She hated everything religious and made threats if anyone offered to pray for her. The director never knew the root cause of her rage and unbelief.

When the woman was dying, she screamed that fire was coming up her legs. It was so bad, the other patients had to be removed from the hallway as she was upsetting other residents. The woman passed away in great anguish.

The sin of this woman's rage and bitterness had infected her children who, in turn, were bitter toward her. One danger of growing an internal root of bitterness is that Paul said the root will defile many (Heb. 12:15), using the analogy of a tree that has roots stretching in all directions. The New Testament Greek word for bitterness is *pikria*, and it can allude to extreme wickedness; producing bitter fruit; bitter hatred. It can also carry a connotation of poison (bitterness is a spiritual poison). The idea is that of pricking something to the point of producing pain. Bitter people carry a wound that leads to unforgiveness and produces bitter fruit.

SINS OF THE FATHERS

God warned that the iniquity of the fathers could be passed to the children, up to the third and fourth generation of those who hate Him (Exod. 34:7). Some have identified this verse with generational curses, teaching that past sins will repeat with future generations. However, the sins of the fathers do not have to be repeated by those who have a personal relationship with Christ. Those who actively follow Christ have been redeemed from the curse of the law, as Christ was made a curse for us (Gal. 3:13).

Once my Italian ancestors repented and followed Christ, their children were raised in church and taught the Bible and the ways of the Lord. They also were taught the danger of alcohol and to avoid it at all costs. That curse was broken because of the power of redemption, forgiveness, and restoration through a relationship with Christ. Their surviving children, John, Joe, Millie, and Caroline, became faithful followers of the Lord.

You and your family members who are redeemed by the blood of Christ can have that same experience. We cannot change the past. However, through a redemptive covenant, we can change the future and our eternal destination.

CHAPTER 4

THE "F" WORD THAT SATAN USES TO HIS ADVANTAGE

T his one word is linked to the ability of the serpent to deceive Adam and Eve. The Jewish historian Josephus noted:

> *"But while all the living creatures had one language, at that time the serpent, which then lived together with Adam and his wife, showed an envious disposition, at his supposal of their living happily, and in obedience to the commands of God; and imagining, that when they disobeyed them, they would fall into calamities, he persuaded the woman, out of a malicious intention..."*

> - *ANTIQUITIES OF THE JEWS*, BOOK 1, CHAPTER 1, SECTION 4)

One condition presents itself as an effective warfare strategy of the enemy, and it very likely was pivotal in the fall of Adam and Eve in the Garden. This can sometimes open doors for the enemy to use the wrong people to create havoc. Adam and Eve had become *comfortable* living with the serpent, who was more crafty and cunning than any beast of the field which God created (Gen. 3:1). The word I'm speaking of is *familiarity*, which creates an environment that has led to countless problems.

Perhaps you have heard the proverbial saying, "familiarity breeds contempt." The phrase is used to explain the human tendency to know someone so well that you stop liking or respecting them because you have seen them exhibit qualities or personality traits that you find undesirable. In other words, the better you know a person, the more you get to know about a person, and the more familiar you become with a person, the more things you find to dislike about that person.

TWO TYPES OF FAMILIAR SPIRITS

The scripture warns us of *familiar spirits*. This is usually described as a demonic spirit that is connected to occult activities. God made it clear that His people must never regard or seek out anyone who operates with a familiar spirit (Lev. 19:31; Deut. 18:10-12). These spirits can operate through wizards, witches, mediums, and people involved in satanic and occult activities.

These spirits become *familiar* with people, places, and events, going back a long time. Familiar spirits can be utilized by alleged psychics when they claim to be consulting the dead. The information these spirits are familiar with concerning the departed person is channeled through the psychic, who then speaks forth the information. Uninformed people believe this is a legitimate act of contacting the spirit of a departed person when, in fact, it is deception. This is a form of sorcery that the Bible refers to as necromancy, which is forbidden by God (Deut. 18:9-12) and was punishable under the Old Testament Law.

Then there is the *familiarity* between unrelated (non-family) individuals who might form emotional "soul ties." Over time, it is possible for people to become so emotionally attached through familiarity that they almost become of one mind. This is similar to the spiritual principle of marriage, when a man and woman are joined together in a covenant and the two become "one flesh" (Gen. 2:24). Paul noted that when a man is joined with a harlot, they become "one body" or "one flesh" (1 Cor. 6:16).

A soul tie attachment can occur with people who work closely together for many years, because as time passes, people become comfortable around each other. They develop trust and share information that they would not tell a mere acquaintance. If people are not careful, this could open a door to a physical attachment, especially if they are spending more time around someone other than their marital companion.

Christian counselors note that Christians at times fall prey to these soul attachments. This generally happens because one person is not getting enough attention or affection at home, so they seek it out with someone they know or trust. Once the familiarity line is crossed, an individual seeking the attention can become both a nuisance and a danger.

A soul-tied individual who is seeking attention or affection often becomes territorial and protective of their relationship or position. They feel threatened by anyone who could take attention away from them or replace them. That's the nuisance level. The danger level comes when that soul-tied individual feels rejected or scorned. Once that happens, emotions explode, and the individual is prone to attack the person with whom they've become familiar—the person who was not supposed to reject them. The worst case scenario is that the rejected person will kill the one doing the rejecting. A more common tactic will be to use their "familiar information" as a weapon.

Beware of forming attachments to these kinds of people. Even perceived attachments can be harmful. To do so can lead to conflicts in business, ministry, and personal life.

If you find yourself being a nuisance in that kind of situation, you can sincerely repent and turn your life around. I heard of a married woman who confessed to her pastor that she was infatuated with a man in the church to whom she was not married. Nothing physical occurred between them, but she constantly fantasized about having a relationship with the man. Once the woman confessed this to God and repented, she experienced freedom and enjoyed a great marriage for many years.

THE INNER CIRCLE

Familiarity occurs more often among those holding an inner circle position. I was raised in a minister's home, and Dad had pastored five different churches by the time I graduated from high school. At age eighteen, I began traveling to preach in different churches, and I almost always stayed in the pastors' homes. Now I'm in my sixties and still preach in different churches. My entire adult life has been built around meeting and developing relationships with countless Christians, pastors, and their church staff. That experience helped me identify three different groups of people found in every ministry and church:

- the *inner circle,* which includes family members, paid staff at the management or supervisory level, and close personal friends;

- the *partners or church members* who love and support the ministry, attend regularly, and volunteer out of love with no expectation for something in return, except perhaps a thank you;

- the *casual attendees* who come when it's convenient or for a special event.

Christ also dealt with three groups of people in His ministry. First, He chose twelve men to be disciples. Of the twelve, Peter, James, and John became Christ's *inner circle*, meaning they were involved with more of the special moments in Christ's life than the other nine men. These three were permitted to see all sides of ministry. They saw the *glory* of the transfiguration and the *gore* of Gethsemane. In one instance, Christ was glowing in the glory (Matt. 17:2). Months later, He was in such agony that His sweat became as great drops of blood (Luke 22:44).

Peter, James, and John could easily handle the triumph of the transfiguration that included Moses and Elijah standing in glory clouds. When the moment of suffering arrived, when Christ stood alone, sweating in agony and knowing that Judas would soon arrive with his strategy of betrayal, even Christ's faithful were prone to scatter. Two of Christ's inner circle disciples covered their own backs for fear that they, too, would be arrested.

At the crucifixion, James was nowhere to be found. Peter hung around for a while, then ran away crying after denying that he knew Christ. Eight other disciples were nowhere to be found. Only one disciple, John, stood fearlessly at the foot of the cross with Christ's mother, Mary (John 19:27).

BETRAYED BY THE FAMILIAR FRIEND

Every person who lives long enough will have a story—some far more damaging than others—that involves inner circle betrayal. I dare say that every pastor I have ever met has a story of an inner circle betrayal that involves someone who left offended, angry, or disappointed in the minister or the ministry.

Why is it that those who are closest are sometimes the quickest to turn against you? There are a few possible reasons. My personal observation is that people often have a pre-conceived expectation about nearly everything. They develop their own fantasies about what it should be like to work in a church or ministry, or even what marriage should be like. In their imaginary world, everybody is happy. Nobody ever disagrees or argues. Angels conduct daily fly-bys to make sure all is perfect. Sudden prayer meetings will erupt, stalling the need to get their work done. And, of course, the ministry leader will be perfect like Jesus.

Eventually, reality sets in. They discover that the people they work with are humans who have good days and bad days. Sometimes they have bad attitudes, and they must deal with other people who have bad attitudes. They are shocked to find that people are imperfect. They have yet to see a single angelic fly-by. The ultimate blow comes when the leader loses his temper, becomes depressed or discouraged, or (heaven forbid!) must correct them. Suddenly they realize their leader is not Jesus, Batman, or the Incredible Hulk. They are emotionally crushed. Their dream job has become a nightmare of disappointment. "This is not what I thought it would be," they bemoan.

UNREALISTIC EXPECTATIONS

In Christ's ministry, His disciples had their own ideas, theories, and expectations tested. The mother of James and John came to Christ privately and asked that her two sons be allowed to sit on His left and right side in the kingdom (Matt. 20:21). The curious disciples asked Christ, "Who is the greatest in the kingdom?" Perhaps they were in a contest to see who could outdo the other for the highest position in the future kingdom. They must have been terribly disappointed when Jesus told them that the greatest in the kingdom is a child (Matt. 18:1-6).

After Christ arose from the dead, these same men posed another big question: "Will you at this time restore the kingdom to Israel?" They had an *expectation* that Christ, the true Messiah, would soon set up God's kingdom and defeat the power of Rome. Together, Christ and His ministry team would rule the world. Christ told them not to focus on restoring the kingdom to Israel, as that was in God's hands. Instead, they should focus on receiving the power of the Holy Spirit (Acts 1:7-8).

These fellows always seemed to miss the main objective and assignment because they were wrapped up in their own pre-conceived ideas and expectations. Jesus had told them He would be killed and raised in three days, yet this revelation went right over their heads until after Christ's resurrection (John 2:19-22).

It is a mistake to place your own expectations on other people. In Acts 12, Herod arrested Peter, threw him in jail, and prepared to execute him after Passover. God interrupted Herod's agenda and sent a delivering angel to release Peter from his chains. The angel opened the closed city gates and led Peter to a house filled with believers who were praying for his release. When Peter physically stood outside the prison, he came to himself and said, "...*Now I know of a surety, that the Lord hath sent his angel, and hath delivered me out of the hand of Herod, and from all the expectation of the people of the Jews*" (Acts 12:11 KJV).

An expectation is a strong anticipation that something will happen in the future. When we stand on God's Word and a promise that we know is from God, we wait in hope and faith with the expectation that we will see the fulfillment. However, we sometimes place unwarranted expectations upon others that often go unfulfilled. That plunges us into discouragement and, eventually, we are out the door. *Excessive familiarity and excessive expectation can lead to excessive disappointment.*

PEOPLE EXPECTED PROPHECY TEACHING

Back in the 1980s after visiting Israel, I was inspired to start teaching on prophecy. Each Saturday night of our revivals, I showed slide pictures from Israel to authenticate where the prophecy was being fulfilled. Soon the Saturday night services became the largest attended and the most requested messages. Over a decade later, prophetic teaching opened a door for the *Manna-Fest* telecast to be taped in Israel with hundreds of programs emphasizing Bible prophecy and the study of our Hebraic roots.

First and foremost, I am an evangelist. I have many other subjects I teach outside of prophecy. However, there was and still is a group of people who only want to hear prophecy, and they attend our meetings with an *expectation* that I will be preaching prophecy. After reading Peter's comment that he was delivered from the "expectation of the people" (Acts 12:11), I set my heart to always follow the leading of the Holy Spirit when I preach. I don't want to concern myself with people becoming upset because I didn't fulfill their sermon expectations.

We can all live in expectation of Christ fulfilling the biblical prophecies, but we must be open to what God desires for us each day and during specific seasons of life. Never be controlled by the fear of other people's expectations.

STAFF INFECTIONS

In medicine, there is something called a *staph infection*. It happens when staphylococcus bacteria invade the body and enter the bloodstream, joints, bones, lungs, or heart. It can become life threatening, and the infected person must get immediate help.

Then there are *staff infections*. This happens when one or more employees of a business or church ministry staff become infected with toxic attitudes or negative opinions, including distorted perceptions about the leadership, church, ministry, and so forth.

For decades I conducted annual revivals in the same churches, usually with the same pastor. When I returned twelve months later, many times a staff member was gone, and a replacement had been hired. There can be several reasons for that. Maybe the person simply decided to take a position elsewhere. Perhaps the person was not suited for the job. However, there were times when the staff member was asked to leave because they sowed discord among other staff or members of the congregation.

All leaders have their own personalities and styles of leadership. However, most will have at least one personality trait that annoys others on staff. Strong personalities often clash. But some people simply have a critical spirit and are constantly on the lookout for something to complain about. I have met a few people who operate off drama, always creating some crisis, blaming someone else, and then claiming they're solving the crisis they created. Mature people settle issues and move on with their day. Immature people thrive on creating chaos and drama.

If ten spies with a negative report can corrupt the faith of over one million Hebrew people by sowing seeds of unbelief that prevented them from inheriting their promised land, then one negative person on staff can defile others on a ministry team or in a church or business.

SIMILARITY VERSUS FAMILIARITY

Researchers have conducted studies that attempt to discover why individuals magnify negative instead of positive traits the more familiar they become with a person. They noticed that relationships begin with *similarity* and often end with *familiarity*.

In these studies, researchers concluded that people connect initially because they have common interests. The more time people spend around each other, the more they see little things they don't like. The more familiar they become with the person—with their beliefs, actions, words, and eccentricities—the more disappointed they can become in the person. Similarity turns to familiarity, and now the person begins to magnify the traits they don't like. They might have entered the relationship with *optimism,* but they depart with *pessimism.*

This happens in relationships and even marriages. The same can happen in a church setting. We join with other believers who have the same values and beliefs. We invite friends to join us and visit this great church with wonderful music, worship, and preaching. We remain loyal until something disappoints us.

Church is a great place to meet likeminded people, and your closest friendships will often be with people you have met at church. But even in a church setting, there will be people you'll get to know because of similarities, and later overfamiliarity will slowly separate you from the person.

Before bailing out of a congregation, think of it like a marriage. A husband and wife may disagree, but if they're determined to keep their marriage together, they do not head to a divorce attorney every time they have a disagreement. They understand that disagreement is part of marriage. We should have the same latitude in the Body of Christ. We can agree to disagree but continue to walk in love instead of offense.

Friendships develop progressively over time: face-to-face, then shoulder-to-shoulder, then back-to-back. First they are acquaintances who talk face-to-face. That might progress to a shoulder-to-shoulder level, as people work together to lift the burdens and loads of the church, ministry, or business. People who appreciate each other and consider themselves good friends learn to stand back-to-back when battles come along. They will protect one another's blind side from backstabbing, verbal assaults, and the spear-throwing of others. In the military they say, "'I've got your six," which simply means, "I have your back." Roman gladiators would fight back-to back, which protected their fellow soldiers from being attacked from behind.

THE ROOT PROBLEM

Christians are accustomed to the habit of telling others, "I love you!" without meaning it or knowing the biblical definition of the word.

According to 1 Corinthians 13, love is patient, kind, not envious, not boastful, not proud, not rude, not self-seeking, not easily angered. Love keeps no record of wrongs, does not delight in evil but rejoices with truth, always protects, always trusts, always hopes, always perseveres. Love has a sacrificial and selfless quality.

Biblical love does not fluctuate with your emotions because it is not based just on your feelings. Biblical love is contrary to natural inclinations, because we know that it is easier to love some people than others. This kind of love Paul wrote of seeks the same welfare for all and seeks to do good to all, especially those who are of the household of faith (Gal. 6:10).

Once someone makes an emotional decision that they no longer love and respect a person, it will nearly always lead to a separation between individuals or, if married, a divorce. This helps explain why some people leave and others stay. The difference between the *leavers* and the *cleavers* is the love that is *gone* or the love that *remains*.

Another problem is the *root of offense*. Unless it is uprooted, offense will produce the fruit of *bitterness*. When offense turns to bitterness, offended individuals will unleash their most powerful weapon— their tongue. An unrestrained tongue is destructive, and that is the why bitter people use it as a knife. They want their loose lips to sink someone else's ship.

Before listening to commentary from a bitter critic, always remember that their side is told from their perspective. There is always another side to every story. Don't let yourself be dragged into someone else's offense and bitterness.

GUARD YOUR HEART

My wife Pam is a very discerning woman. She once warned me about keeping my guard up and not letting certain people get close because of their motives. She said, "You trust some people to your own detriment. They will use you, get what they want, and then turn on you." I have learned by experience that she knows what she is talking about. It pays to pay attention.

Guarding your heart includes maintaining a safe barrier against the wrong people. Not everybody should be part of your inner circle. Not everybody needs to be "in the loop," including those who try to push their way into your life because they see a potential benefit for themselves. Sometimes this lesson has to be learned the hard way.

Most ministers desire that their family become their closest employees in the ministry. Moses set the pattern. His brother Aaron was the first high priest. His father-in-law, Jethro, assisted Moses with counselling responsibilities. Moses' sister, Mariam, was part of a worship team who sang and rejoiced at the Red Sea. Moses selected Joshua, a loyal man for forty years, to become his personal assistant. My wife, my son Jonathan, my daughter Amanda, and my daughter-in-law Katie all work in ministry.

Maintain awareness of the potential to move from *similarity* to *familiarity*. It is not always easy to discern the motives and hidden intent of people who try to gain closer access to us. Sometimes we need the eyes of trustworthy people in our lives to warn us. That includes being willing to accept a warning from family and friends about someone you are dating who could potentially become a spouse. Don't let yourself get caught in the emotionalism of similarity and discover too late that you are caught in a trap.

Another reason to guard your heart is because whatever thoughts possess your heart will eventually manifest visibly. Sin originates in the imagination and the heart. If you do not continue the path of renewal and transformation of your mind and heart, eventually you can be pulled away from righteous living.

THE REMNANT IS SMALL

A great man of God who had a global ministry before he died at an advanced age told a fellow minister that, if you come to the end of your life and can count on one hand the number of people who remained your true friend and never betrayed or hurt you, then you have done well.

For me personally, I have lived much of my day-to-day life working in an office alone. Since my teen years and during seasons throughout my life, I have battled depression that included a desire to isolate myself. I was just fine having only one friend at a time. Even now, I have an office that is away from ministry activities and employees. Besides myself, only four men and my wife can access the security features of my office. I appreciate my staff and the great work they do, but I choose to work alone in a quiet setting. When traveling, if Pam cannot go, then one or two men travel with me. I keep my inner circle very small, limited to a few men who are longtime trusted friends and my wife Pam, who is my best friend and closest confidant.

In the biblical account of David's life, he organized six hundred mighty men who formed the top tier of his military staff. Within that group were thirty-three who were superior to others in battle. Of that thirty-three, only three men stood as outstanding above the others and were considered David's most powerful mighty men. Only three out of six hundred. While all the men were willing to fight alongside David, the stunning military feats of only three were unsurpassed in all of Israel. His best fighters became his inner circle (2 Sam. 23).

Jesus selected seventy people to minister two-by-two throughout Israel (Luke 10:1). He chose and trained twelve men who would one day take the Gospel to the world. Peter, one of His three inner circle disciples, became the chief apostle of the Jewish branch of the church (Paul led the Gentile branch). James became the director in Jerusalem, the headquarters of the church.

A valuable lesson I especially want to impart to other ministers is that it is good to have people whom you consider good friends. But keep your *inner-circle* small. Honor and remain close to those who stand with you during your most difficult times. Pam and I are grateful for the many friends we have in ministry. However, I have known only a few men throughout my life who would stand with me in both the best and worst of times. Those who hold up your arms in the battle are the ones of whom it is written, "A friend loves at all times" (Prov. 17:17).

BECOMING FAMILIAR WITH FAMILY WEAKNESSES

Most families will have some type of weight, sin, or weakness that surfaces from generation to generation. It is possible to become so familiar with these weights or sins, that you slowly accept them as part of your life or view them as family DNA that is part of your gene pool. *You will never attempt to rid yourself of anything negative that you have accepted as part of your life.*

When my wife was a young girl, her mother experienced a nervous breakdown. She and her two sisters stayed with her father and stepmother, but that did not work out. Eventually all three girls were invited to live in the home of a wonderful family from church. When Pam and I were married, even though her father lived a few miles from the church, he never showed up to the wedding.

Pam could have chosen to play the role of a victim who was rejected and live in anger toward her father. I once asked her, "You turned out to be an amazing wife, mother, and grandmother. You are positive and happy, full of love, and family oriented. How did you not end up bitter because of your past?" She answered, "I chose a long time ago not to live in my past but to live for my future."

A minister said, "Eternal life is a free gift from God, but abundant life is a choice" (John 10:10). Eternal life is God's gift to us. An abundant, joyful life is your gift back to God for His goodness.

An abundant life is a choice when you enter a redemptive covenant, draw closer to God, and become more familiar with Him and His Word. Paul said, "That I may know Him…" (Phil. 3:10). No prudence is necessary when becoming *familiar* with God.

CHAPTER 5

BREAKING A GENERATIONAL PORNOGRAPHY SPIRIT

If several generations in one family battle pornographic addiction, some would suggest it is a generational curse. However, I suggest it can be a familiar spirit operating in a family linage, causing some to be stuck in a cycle of fleshly bondage. These spirits try to capitalize on a family weakness or stronghold. Once the weakness becomes a bondage, the familiar spirits will return and attempt to trap other family members into that same bondage.

In my family, a pornographic spirit manifested twice with a separation of forty-two years when it attacked two young minds, both of whom were eleven years of age when it happened.

In my situation, our family had moved to Northern Virginia. This region of the state was far different culturally and spiritually from the rural mountain town of Big Stone Gap, Virginia, the place we moved from that had a population at that time of around 4,500.

Our family lived in a neighborhood of small homes in Arlington (population then was around 175,000), located just outside Washington, D.C. The houses were so close together that if a neighboring family argued, nearby neighbors could be standing in their yards and hear every detail of the fiery disagreement.

One day, two friends and I were playing and running through the woods behind our homes when we came upon a garbage bag. Curious, we opened it to discover a stash of pornographic magazines, which was something I had never seen. We thumbed through the pages and slid them back into the garbage bag. We agreed not to tell anybody what we had found, and we would start a "playboy club."

For several weeks, we headed to the woods to our hidden location. For us at the time, we considered this a secret between friends and not some type of perversion we were engaged in. We were kids thinking this was fun. *That, of course, is what the enemy wanted us to think.* The Bible warns that sin creates a pleasure for a season, but the negative consequences can linger a lifetime (Heb.11:25).

I don't remember how long we kept the magazines hidden, but eventually they were discovered by someone, and the plastic bag disappeared. Thankfully, I never came under bondage to pornography, perhaps because that same summer, I was baptized in the Holy Spirit at a church youth camp in Virginia. That spiritual infilling caused me to experience a renewed mind and a desire for God's presence at a young age.

FORWARD FORTY-TWO YEARS

My wife and I were unaware that the same spirit (perhaps a familiar spirit) returned forty-two years later to target our eleven-year-old daughter. Statistics indicate that the average age of a child's first exposure to porn today happens before the age of eleven. Today they don't have to discover magazines in the woods. They can simply stumble upon it because they are online.

The mental assault against our daughter was exposed when she was fifteen. Our ministry was hosting Warrior-Fest, and Amanda was on the church drama team. During the conference my wife Pam approached me and said, "Perry, Amanda is going to say something this morning publicly that happened to her and she's afraid of how you will react."

I said, "What is it?"

Pam replied, "She didn't tell me, but she's afraid you'll be upset or disappointed in her." Many questions rushed through my mind all at once. What in the world had she done?

The moment came for her to testify before the drama team ministered. She confessed that at age eleven, she saw pornography on an iPad and became addicted. She expressed how she would repent and go back to watching it, repent again and go back, until finally one night, alone in her bedroom after a church service, she cried out to God and told Him that she was tired of this bondage and wanted to be free.

The Almighty *instantly* gave her a spiritual and mental deliverance and told her to pray and dive into reading the Word. It took boldness for her to stand up and admit this publicly in front of several thousand young people and adults. That night I told her that I was not upset with her, and I told her about my story that happened at age eleven.

The same type of attack happening at the same age and in the same family is not a coincidence. It was a set-up for bondage, with the enemy hoping we would become caged in a metal prison with a porn addiction that would build strongholds that would be difficult to break.

THE EARLY DAYS OF MY FATHER

When I was a young man, my dad told me several stories as examples of spiritual warnings. When he was in his mid-teens, some of his relatives were moonshiners, which led to alcohol abuse. He said that when he and a few other guys in the family were young teenagers, one of the older men used one of the barns as a place to drink moonshine and seduce local women. Since biblical times, drunkenness and nudity seem to go together, as seen after the flood with Noah (Gen.

9:21). When people are drunk, they often lose control of their senses and their discipline. That includes having an unrestrained mouth, no ability to control their actions, and a lack of moral restraint.

Dad recalled an occasion when this loose living relative told a few of the teen-age guys to go hide in the barn and "watch the show." This is perverse and evil. Yet, even decades ago, such activity was not unheard of, especially among the unsaved. In some instances, children were born into a family where the assumed father was not the actual father. People might suspect a different father, but it wasn't discussed in polite company.

GENERATIONAL WEAKNESSES

We can observe how certain bondages and strongholds seem to pass from one generation to the next. Abraham, Isaac, Jacob, and his sons all had occasions where they told lies. There are families in which almost every family member transgressed into some form of sexual sin, including on both sides of the family. For some, they succumbed to temptation and repented, never repeating the act again. For others, it became a lifetime bondage that might not have been confessed and repented of until they were on their death beds, if at all.

Temptation has been around since the fall of Adam and Eve. Three heroes of ancient Israel—Samson, David, and Solomon—brought grief and frustration upon themselves because of a weakness for women. Samson was attracted to numerous Philistine beauties, including harlots in Gaza (Judges 16:1). His actions drove him into the hands of Delilah, who provided a free haircut that severed the last of his Nazarite vows and cost Samson his strength and anointing (Judges 14-16).

We know the story of David and Bathsheba, but you might not know that David married eight wives who birthed a total of eighteen children. Most of them were born before he was crowned Israel's king.

David's son Solomon was obsessed with signing trade agreements with every tribe and nation. He sealed the deals by entering marital arrangements with seven hundred wives who eventually turned his heart away from God (1 Kings 11:3). This record-breaking harem was not normal in that culture. In fact, the law of God instructed future Israelite kings not to multiply wives (Deut. 17:17), noting that their foreign religious beliefs would turn the king toward idolatry, which was Solomon's downfall.

THE PONEROS FACTOR

In the New Testament is a Greek word *poneros* which is translated *evil*. The word *porne* is prostitute, and *porneia* is the Greek word for *fornication*. Pornography can and often does lead to other forms of sexual sins, including prostitution and acts such as fornication, adultery, and even rape. Studies show that pornography addictions ruin relationships, degrade self-worth, and change perceptions of life, people, and reality.

Pornography has a similar effect on the brain as cocaine. Outside of the cravings for certain foods that are impossible for some to resist (such as chocolate), the emotions and feelings attached to sexual activity—including pornography—are some of the most aggressive and difficult to discipline. This is because these activities release "feel good" chemicals in the brain—dopamine, serotonin, oxytocin, and endorphins—which play a role in many bodily functions. Dopamine is the reward center that affects memory, mood, and motivation. Serotonin helps regulate mood, sleep, and digestion. Endorphins are natural pain relievers in response to stress and discomfort. Oxytocin promotes strong parent-child bonding and promotes trust and empathy.

Engaging in certain everyday activities will activate these chemicals. Activities such as exercise, spending time outdoors, working in a garden, listening to music or playing a musical instrument, eating certain foods, laughing, spending time with close friends, and owning a pet all help activate these necessary chemicals.

Unacceptable activities will also activate these chemicals. Illegal drug use is a great example. Some people get a chemical rush from engaging in dangerous sports activities.

Viewing pornography also activates a chemical release, which is a serious problem in our modern culture. People, including young people, who should be releasing brain chemicals by engaging in acceptable activities choose instead to engage in unacceptable and sinful activities. This affects their spiritual lives, relationships, and marriages.

The chemical rush makes it difficult for them to distinguish between true love and carnal lust. They think they're in love, and when the relationship ends and the chemical rush stops, depression and hopelessness kick in. Young people have harmed themselves and even committed suicide because they cannot handle the hopeless feelings they experience after a relationship breakup.

A hidden addiction to pornography will ruin marriages, which happens more often than reported. Couples divorce because the wife discovers the husband's hidden porn addiction. Instead of repenting and taking the necessary steps to reverse the addiction, the husband would rather go through a divorce and move on to the next woman. He will schmooze the next woman while hiding his addiction, then go through the same cycle if he remarries.

When these chemicals wash over the frontal lobe of the brain, they can eventually overpower mental reasoning. The addiction to the feeling will cause people to act irrationally and do things that are risky.

Access to pornography is too easy for anybody with internet access, regardless of age. The computer or smartphone doesn't care about the person's age. It's up to parents to use filters, blocks, and passwords on electronic devices, but even that is no guarantee of protection.

Practically speaking, there are simple self-control options that will help prevent someone from falling into the bondage of pornography. First, *seal off the pipeline.* Cut off the source, whether it be your phone, the movies you watch, or your friends who are leading you down this dangerous path. Once someone becomes addicted to pornography, it becomes more difficult for them to give it up. Your best option is to stay away from it entirely and never open the door to bondage.

Researchers are now suggesting something that Bible-believing Christians have known all along. The way out of a pornography addiction is through faith and moral clarity that provide for and encourage higher standards of behavior. As you set your heart to focus on God's Word, as you grow in your faith, as your moral behavior changes, and as you purposefully focus on higher-level cognition, all of that will help override your desire to focus solely on yourself and activities that feed your own flesh.

The pornography addict must come to a decision-making crossroad and realize that the addiction is a war against their soul. Then the addict needs some type of accountability, a person close to them who checks up on how they are doing and encourages them to continue in freedom. The third party will help cut the root of any temptation, such as movie channels or access online.

If you are married and dealing with this bondage, it is important to have the kind of relationship with your spouse where you can be open with each other if you are pressured to yield to anything that would be destructive to your spiritual walk. Also, understand the chemical component within the brain that is activated when viewing pornographic images. This is what causes addiction, just as with drugs or even food.

Gaining freedom is a choice and a decision, not chance or luck. It is the will of God that you have power, love and a sound mind (2 Tim. 1:7).

CHAPTER 6

TAKE A RIDE IN THE HILLS OR A RIDE IN A HEARSE

If you are a self-motivated workaholic who survives on lack of sleep, here is something you must learn. In the West, Sunday is the traditional Sabbath. Pastors and ministers work on the Sabbath because church services are held on the Sabbath, so this instruction is also important for us. The consequences of not following this biblical instruction of a day of rest could send you to heaven sooner than you expect. It is important to take time off to rest, restore, and refresh your mind and body.

In May of 2020, after a battery of medical tests, a doctor instructed me to change my lifestyle, including reducing stress, or before long I could drop dead in my office. A second physician asked me if I was interested in staying alive long enough to attend my daughter's wedding. Both motivated me to change many unhealthy patterns.

THE SABBATH IS NOT OPTIONAL

Many people spend time arguing over the true Sabbath day while missing the main point, which is the *purpose* of the day—to cease from labor. There was a practical and spiritual purpose for why God established the seventh day as a day of rest. In the King James translation of the Bible, the word Sabbath is important enough to be mentioned 137 times. The Hebrew word means "to repose; to cease from labor; to rest." The Sabbath was first established when God rested on the seventh day of creation (Gen. 2:2). When the Israelites lived in Egypt as slaves, it is believed they worked seven days a week performing tasks such as making bricks for the construction of Pharaoh's treasure cities.

After the Israelites left Egypt, God revealed to Moses His rules that we know as the Ten Commandments. One commandment is that people and animals are to rest and be free from labor on the seventh day (Exodus 20:9-11). In ancient Israel, every seventh year was marked as a sabbatical year, called a *shmita*, where the land would not be cultivated, thereby allowing it to rest from sowing and pruning (Lev. 25:3-5). Seven Sabbaths of years led to the year of Jubilee, marked as the fiftieth year. This is a time when people were not to cultivate land and where personal debt was released (Lev. 25:8-11). The poor could come to the fields and gather food during the seventh year, and anything that remained could be eaten by the animals (Exod. 23:11).

Jews and Messianic believers observe the Sabbath beginning on Friday before sunset and ending on Saturday after nightfall. Traditional Protestants, Catholics, and Orthodox Christians observe the Sabbath on Sunday ("the first day of the week"), as that became the day when Gentile Christians gathered (Matt. 28:1; Acts 20:7; 1 Cor. 16:2).

Ministers don't rest on this day, as they are normally preaching and serving in the church on Sunday, often in multiple services. Some ministers take off on Monday. When I was growing up, most churches conducted Sunday school, a morning church service, and another service on Sunday night. As a pastor, for many years my dad had to work a secular job to make ends meet, while also being on call seven days a week to take care of various duties at the church and assist church members. For the early years of my life in Southwestern Virginia, Dad was the pastor, church greeter, custodian, and the man who kept coal in the church furnace during the winter.

Jesus noted that the Sabbath day was made for man and not man for the Sabbath (Mark 2:27). I think God rested on the seventh day because there was nothing left on His list to create! God does not become physically tired and He neither slumbers nor sleeps (Psa. 121:4). He rested and set an example for us.

MY SIN AGAINST THE SABBATH

For decades, we had only the Voice of Evangelism ministry. Then the Omega Center International facility was built. The International School of the Word Bible College was developed after that, which placed a greater demand and expectation upon me—not by the Lord, but by myself and by people. Over time, the ministry costs just to cover expenses leaped from hundreds of thousands of dollars a year to over millions of dollars a year. At age eighteen, I committed to not sending letters asking for financial support, which required trusting God alone for all ministry income.

As the staff and the budget grew, I felt the pressure on myself to be financially responsible for the staff salaries, plus their insurance and other benefits, along with project financing and the maintenance and upkeep of all the properties. As an evangelist who traveled almost every weekend and sometimes during the week, I also felt a strong burden for the millions of people I ministered to globally. All ministers and ministries have a great responsibility to be good stewards of what God has given and to prudently spread the Gospel to the audience God has placed before them.

Before I realized what was happening, I was consumed with non-stop work to the point of ignoring God's Sabbath laws. Even at the ancient temple, the Levites served in cycles, with breaks between work seasons. But for years, I was stuck in my own rut of nonstop studying, preaching, traveling, writing, taping, and caring for ministry needs.

During the ten years leading up to the time the government restricted church gatherings because of covid fears, we had built the 72,000-square-foot Omega Center International, which opened for our first conference in 2013. We built the lodge that housed offices and special gatherings and now houses Nik Walker Ministries and will house our Holy Land relic museum. We made improvements to our television studio and purchased new equipment. I wrote a million-word commentary of the Bible that took seven years, prepared an average of one-hundred-fifty messages a year for conferences and speaking engagements, and preached five or six messages a weekend during our conferences.

Our annual trip to Israel required researching and writing forty new messages to be prepared in advance for on-site *Manna-fest* program taping. The other half of the *Manna-Fest* messages had to be prepared and taped in the studio. From mid-2015 until 2020, I preached almost every week at our Tuesday night services at Omega Center. Throughout the year I recorded CDs and DVDs as resource material to help with television expenses. We hosted several conferences a year at OCI, including two Warrior-Fests. I wrote anywhere between two and five new books a year. I prepared articles for the Voice of Evangelism magazine which is produced quarterly. Once the International School of the Word was organized, I researched and taught courses, some with eighty pages of outlines. Voice of Evangelism was responsible for staff and the upkeep of every building, plus 110 acres of property.

My main point in telling you this is to show you that I worked too many hours a day, seven days a week. I took only one vacation a year with my family. That time was often spent writing a book, instead of spending time with family.

RESOURCE ORIENTED MINISTRY

An evangelistic ministry never has a guarantee of a certain amount of income. The Lord has provided all along, but I still felt pressure and responsibility hanging over my head for all this. All ministries and churches depend on funds coming in from somewhere. The sources for income are tithes, offerings, projects, and teaching materials. God doesn't plant a money tree in anybody's back yard; He provides through the obedience of people so He can bless the ones who obediently give. Some who support do so as a *seed*; others give to meet a *need*, while others give to perform a good *deed* for God's Kingdom. Our ministry and many others like ours have a partner base. However, much of the VOE income is derived from resource materials that we make available for purchase. As costs increased, new teaching resources were required to help keep our *Manna-Fest* telecast on the air globally.

Years ago, I told my wife that I never want to preach to pay salaries and ministry bills. I want to preach because I have a word from God; not to pay expenses. But I found myself having to do the very thing I never desired to do.

For a decade, I would come home late, eat dinner, then work past midnight writing or doing research. I had no life outside of ministry work. When the rest of the family was enjoying themselves, I was working. My sweet wife never complained and never even rebuked me except to say, "Perry, you need to take a break. You're operating off adrenaline. One day you'll collapse, and God will make you take a break." I nodded in agreement as I continued typing away on my laptop.

It was wrong not to take one day a week to rest and refresh my body and mind. I was so consumed with the work of the ministry and the responsibility for other people that I felt guilty if I wasn't doing something ministry related. In my way of thinking, doing nothing was wasting God's time, and I thought of that as a sin against the Kingdom of God. Yet, I did not follow the law of the Sabbath or enjoy its purpose.

IT SUDDENLY HAPPENED

Just as Pam warned, the nonstop work caught up with me. In January of 2020, a couple months before the unexpected public announcement that the government was going to shut down nearly everything because of a virus, I was at the office sitting at my desk. I got up to walk to a table, when suddenly all strength left my body, my knees buckled, and I found myself lying on the floor. I was like a glove after the hand is removed. Too weak to get up, I stayed on the floor with a Bible under my head. This was followed by weeks of intense brain fog. I could not recall small details. This was becoming so common that it concerned me.

The weakness, added to various uncontrollable circumstances that included nationwide covid lockdowns, caused a forced sabbatical. This happened at a time when access to clinics and hospitals had virtually been shut down because the entire world feared covid. My wife learned of one clinic, far away from home, that was available for treatment. I received a month of both medical treatment and intense counseling sessions to deal with the root of being a workaholic. Every medical test I received came back with a bad report—blood pressure, blood sugar, heart, A1C, everything. My arteries were forming calcium deposits, which could lead to heart problems.

The doctor at the clinic said he was surprised I wasn't on the floor with a stroke. When he told me how close I could be to dying within a few years, he had my attention. I had come to the end of myself and now was forced to make choices that meant life or death.

MINISTRY TRANSITIONS

Pam, close friends, ministry leaders, and I felt it necessary to release myself from the responsibilities of two of the ministries. One was the International School of the Word (ISOW), housed in a wonderful facility that was once the T.L. Lowery Global Foundation Ministry Center. Dr. Bryan Cutshall, a brilliant and highly capable man of God who has trained over twenty thousand ministers, took over the school, which has over ten thousand students taking classes online. Voice of Evangelism owns the building, while Dr. Cutshall is President of the school and is doing an outstanding job. He also began overseeing the global prayer service that is livestreamed from ISOW every Thursday night.

The Omega Center International was placed under the supervision of The Ramp, the ministry of Karen Wheaton. Eventually Dr. Cutshall agreed to become the lead pastor of the Ramp in Cleveland. In 2024, Karen Wheaton and her husband Rick turned the responsibility back to us to fulfill the original vision given when it was built. Before our head intercessor died in 2024 at the age of ninety-two, she also gave me a word from the Lord that we must return to the original vision. This spacious and impressive facility continues to host our annual conferences, numerous guest ministry events, and the weekly Tuesday night services, where the highly capable Dr. Cutshall remains the campus pastor.

THE FINAL OUTCOME

During almost fifty years of ministry, many of my transitions happened suddenly and unexpectedly. When spiritual warfare was involved, at times it felt like a well-orchestrated strategy designed in the war room of darkness as a satanically inspired plot to force me into a corner of discouragement and silence. In July of 2023, I preached in Montana and was forced to cut the meeting short due to sickness. I came home and was diagnosed with pneumonia and strep throat, and my temperature went to 106. It was another physical attack. Following this, a strong weakness set into my body that continued for months.

I encountered a long, drawn-out season of resetting my life patterns, work, and travel schedule. The book of Job teaches us that God used Satan to His advantage in the larger scheme that led to Job's double portion breakthrough. Satan thought he was in command of events and thought he knew the outcome of his strategy, which was to make Job curse God (Job 1:11; 2:5). However, Satan was only a pawn on God's chessboard. *Satan knows it is impossible to put the King in checkmate on God's own chess board.*

During every test, trial, and crisis, the Holy Spirit kept giving me, my wife, and our ministry partners the same scripture. After Joseph was thrown in a pit, sold as a slave, accused by Potiphar's wife, and jailed for almost thirteen years under false charges, he was suddenly released to a position in Pharaoh's palace as a seer (dream interpreter). He later told his brothers, "You meant evil against me, but God meant it for good" (Gen. 50:20).

In retrospect, God was allowing a chastisement to me personally. It took many months to reset, restore, and be refreshed after laying aside the work of ministry and listening to His still small voice.

This experience taught me to take breaks from work. Ministers should take time away from ministry, staff, the congregation, and their occupation. I have written a commentary on the Bible. I have written over a hundred books and booklets, recorded thousands of messages and hundreds of CDs and DVDs, and hosted many conferences. If I pass away before Christ's return, everything that seemed so important while I was alive will be sold in yard sales, donated to thrift stores, or thrown away. My name will be a memory, mentioned occasionally by a few who outlive me. What will remain on earth will be a few relatives recalling my life. I have worked hard, long hours and will continue to work while I can. But I will work wiser and smarter, not harder. And I will enjoy the atmosphere of God's rest.

MY INSTRUCTION TO YOU

Here are some lifestyle changes that helped me. They might also help you live longer, be more joyful, and live life with more internal peace.

1. Take Brief Rests

An elderly minister said that, when he turned sixty-five, he took a short nap in the afternoon that helped renew his strength for the church services at night. I decided to try that. Now I arrive at work about the same time as my employees, or at times a bit earlier or later. After lunch, I lie down to rest and pray. I don't often fall asleep, but I rest. I listen to outdoor nature sounds on my laptop and stop working for at least thirty minutes. Some call this a siesta, the idea of which is rooted in the culture of Spain. Originally, it gave farmers a break from the hot afternoon sun and renewed their energy to finish the day. Eventually the siesta became a staple of the culture.

When Christ was tired, He slept. He would go aside and rest with His disciples and remove Himself from the pressure of the people (Mark 6:31). Christ ministered to the point of exhaustion and then fell asleep in a boat while a storm was erupting on the Sea of Galilee (Matt. 8:24).

Take a power nap. When T.L. Lowery was traveling to preach, he would ask someone to drive his car. He instructed the driver, "Don't speak to me for the next fifteen to thirty minutes." He would sit up, shut his eyes, and take a brief nap. When he awoke, he said it was as though he had slept a few hours. This was one of his secrets to renewing his mind and body when he ministered in his senior years. He still traveled and preached into his early 80s.

The famous inventor Thomas Edison used a similar method. As you grow older, take a brief power nap every day at some point. Fifteen to twenty minutes is said to help and has been shown to refresh the brain and boost alertness without entering a deep sleep stage. The short nap resets the body's systems.

2. Get Up and Move

For years I was glued to a laptop, and many days I didn't take a lunch break. When I did, someone either brought lunch to my desk where I ate and continued working, or I ate food that wasn't a healthy choice. I have since made better choices.

Sitting all day is not healthy for many reasons. Today, even though I'm still sitting behind a desk and typing on a laptop, I work for a while, then get up and walk around, lift hand weights, or go to other areas to check on ministry activities and updates. I make myself get up and move, and sometimes I walk inside the buildings for exercise.

Doctors say that sitting all day without exercise is as dangerous to the physical body as smoking. Sitting all day can increase the likelihood of becoming overweight, developing type 2 diabetes and heart disease, or experiencing depression and anxiety. Walking outdoors in the sunshine increases vitamin D, which is lacking in most adults who don't spend time outdoors in the sun. Walk as much as possible and stand up periodically to stretch if you sit at a desk all day.

3. Find a Fun Hobby

This was another area of weakness for me. Many people play golf. I attempted this on a few occasions, but it ended with me walking around the green frustrated. I decided I didn't want to attempt any sport that I had no chance of ever winning. Many men love the woods and hunting. I tried that years ago but found it challenging to shoot a deer that stared at me with big brown eyes. I do enjoy fishing in the coastal areas but seldom have the chance. Nobody in my family plays sports, so our family activities primarily revolve around church.

I had collected sports cards for a long time, and then started collecting ancient biblical coins. When I need a mental break, I drive to a sports card shop and hang out with the guys and *talk* about sports. Other times I work on coin sets. Both hobbies occasionally bring in personal income.

A hobby is not just for the sake of having something fun to do. A hobby can also be a stress reliever. When I start to get mentally overloaded, this gives me a reason to get up for a bit and leave the work behind.

4. Take a short trip.

Our ministry currently conducts three conferences a year at OCI. People set aside the time and income to attend these events, as they are encouraging, informative, life changing, and can be a lot of fun. But some people never leave home and never take a trip just for the fun of it.

One of the ways I clear my mind is to drive through the mountains and listen to gospel music. I have three favorite locations, and throughout the year, I set aside a few days to visit these places and fellowship with family and friends. Pam and I enjoy driving and eating together at a certain restaurant.

Taking short trips, even day trips, will break the routine of life and give you something to look forward to. You don't have to go far or spend a lot of money. Pam and I have three grandchildren who live next door, and they come over to see Nana almost every day. Sometimes we take them on a trip to Pigeon Forge. Other times Pam and I take a trip alone with no family tagging along. We have a date dinner once a week. If you are married, you need time together, just the two of you. The day will come when these trips will be recalled as fond memories.

All the above are lifestyle changes I made by *choice* because of physical, mental, and spiritual necessity. Your choices become your daily patterns, and your patterns become your routine. Negative routines become ruts and are difficult to change. But you must make changes that are best for your mental, physical, and spiritual well-being. Take a break, rest, get healthy, enjoy life, and live longer. *Your ability to rest and take a Sabbath could determine if your next drive will be to worship at the church or ride in the back of a hearse.*

CHAPTER 7

NOT FLESH AND BLOOD BUT A DARK ANGELIC PRINCE

Paul the apostle wrote to the church of Ephesus and said something that doesn't always make sense to someone who has been engaged in serious conflicts that involve belligerent and downright evil individuals. Paul told the believers, "For we wrestle not against flesh and blood..." (Eph. 6:12).

This appears to be a contradiction because, throughout Paul's life, he was constantly hindered, harassed, lied on, and abused by flesh and blood human beings. After his conversion, leaders in Damascus plotted to kill him. He was forced to escape over the city wall in a basket tied to ropes (Acts 9:25). He was stoned by Jewish haters of the gospel in Lystra and left in the dust for dead (Acts 14:19). He was arrested by Roman guards, persecuted by religious fanatics, and run out of town by screaming mobs stirred by angry idol worshippers. He was beaten with rods. With all this documented warfare instigated by people, how can Paul say that our struggle is not with flesh and blood?

Second Corinthians 12:7 answers this enigma. Paul exposed a personal invisible enemy he identified as a "thorn in the flesh," which he called a "messenger of Satan." The Greek word *messenger* is translated as *angel*. Paul understood that this evil angel was "a ruler of the darkness of this world," and a "wicked spirit in heavenly places" (Eph.

6:12). He received a divine revelation that this angel of Satan had been assigned to work against his ministry by inspiring religious fanatics to resist his preaching; by forcing city officials to arrest him and have him scourged or imprisoned; and by creating difficult circumstances that could have led to Paul's premature death.

Christians can suddenly experience a fiery dart being shot into their minds by demonic powers. Satan entered the heart of Judas (Luke 22:3). Christ rebuked Peter for speaking a statement contrary to God's will. Christ responded to Peter with, "Get behind Me, Satan" (Matt. 16:23). Ananias and his wife Sapphira, members of the Jerusalem church, sold property and conspired to withhold finances they promised the church. Peter scolded them and exposed how Satan had filled their hearts to lie to the Holy Spirit (Acts 5:3). The lesson here is that Christians can yield their minds and mouths to an evil spirit without discerning the true source that is inspiring their actions.

THE SUDDEN AMBUSH

Of twelve Apostles (eleven, if we omit Judas), why did Peter seem to always be at the top of Satan's hit list? The answer may be found in a prophecy that Christ spoke over him.

When Peter confessed that Jesus was the Son of the Living God, Jesus publicly acknowledged Peter's remarks as an inspired revelation from His Heavenly Father. Christ immediately told Peter, *"And I will give to you the keys of the kingdom of heaven; and whatsoever you bind on earth will be bound in heaven, and whatever you loose on earth will be loosed in heaven"* (Matt. 16:19).

Three verses later, Peter rebuked Christ for warning His disciples that He would die in Jerusalem (Matt. 16:20-22). It appears that Satan heard this entire conversation, including Peter's revelation of Christ being God's Son and even Peter's rebuke of Christ.

Weeks later, Christ perceived that a satanic ambush was being set up to wreck Peter's confidence and destroy his faith. Christ warned Peter that *"Satan has desired to have you, that he may sift you as wheat"* (Luke 22:31). This word *desired* alludes to demanding or begging earnestly for something. Sifting was the process of removing the chaff and small stones from the wheat after is it crushed. At the Temple, the wheat was sifted through ten different processes to ensure that the flour was pure. Sifting Peter as wheat would *prove him* by testing if he would collapse or stand under pressure.

The purpose of Peter's test was to crush his personal faith so he would become disappointed with his failure, which would cause him to quit the ministry and forfeit his God ordained future to be the head of the Jewish branch of the church. Without an apostle overseeing the Jewish converts, the church would be weakened and possibly divided.

Indeed, Peter failed by falling into the enemy's trap. He slept in Gethsemane when Jesus was in agony. He woke up suddenly and assaulted the high priest's servant with a sword. Out of fear, three times Peter lied and denied even knowing Christ. He placed a self-curse upon himself (he cursed an oath) to impress his accusers that he was not a Christ follower and did not know Him (Matt. 26:72). Jesus predicted that through this attack, Peter would be converted—a word meaning "to revert, to return again." Peter would fail but would also be restored.

THE MYSTERY OF THE EAR

Perhaps Peter feared that he would be arrested as Christ had been. He also may have feared being charged with assaulting the high priest's servant. In Gethsemane, Peter had been willing to die for Christ, and he proved his loyalty by cutting off the right ear of Malchus (John 18:10). Jesus destroyed all evidence against Peter through a creative miracle by restoring the ear as though nothing happened.

This act of restoring the ear conceals a hint of prophecy. Peter's name was Simon, which in Hebrew means "listen" or "hear." The right ear on a high priest represented the priest's ability to hear from God. His ear was anointed with blood (Exod. 29:20). Peter had a *hearing* problem. Jesus would teach and instruct him, yet at times he would do his own thing. He was abrupt, quick to speak, and a bit prideful. Peter sliced off the right ear of a man, yet Jesus destroyed the evidence of a crime by healing and restoring the man's ear. Peter's challenge was *hearing and listening* to instruction. After being separated from Christ by a satanic ambush, Peter would be restored by Christ Himself.

The restoration process began when Peter came to his senses and realized he had done the wrong thing and was not an effective listener. It requires a spiritual ear to hear the insights the Spirit is releasing (Rev. 2:7). All restoration from sin, disobedience, or failure begins with realizing you said or did the wrong thing. Notice Peter's reaction once he realized his actions were a betrayal: "And he went out and wept bitterly" (Matt. 26:75). He did not just weep sad tears; he wept bitterly. Bitterly is *pikros* in Greek, and the word means more than just crying. It means to sob uncontrollably. His heart and spirit were broken because of his betrayal.

Christ was led to Golgotha and crucified at nine o'clock in the morning (the third hour). He passed away at three o'clock in the afternoon (the ninth hour). Peter was not present at the crucifixion scene, and neither were any other disciples except John, as each disciple feared for his own life.

Three days later, Peter and John ran to the tomb to confirm Christ's resurrection. Later, Christ met the disciples at the Sea of Galilee, where Jesus restored Peter back into the ministry and commissioned him to feed the flock of believers (John 21:17).

Peter preached the first sermon at Pentecost and saw three thousand Jews come to Messiah (Acts 2:41). Later, Peter connected the

Jewish believers with the new Gentile converts (Acts 10). As the primary spiritual leader among converted Jews, Peter's significance for the church cannot be underestimated.

RESTORATION RESISTERS

From Genesis 3:15 to Revelation 21:1, when God finally restores the earth back to its original Garden of Eden nature, the entire Bible holds stories of covenants, redemption, and restoration. Throughout church history, Christian leaders have sometimes fallen prey to traps of the adversary, which brought a temporary or permanent halt to their ministry activities. Western church denominations have special committees and most ministries have a board of elders to resolve situations or investigate allegations against their spiritual leaders. The leader might be required to step aside for a season and receive whatever help is required that leads to restoration.

Oddly, you'll find a few people, including a few ministers, who teach that an erring minister should never be restored to ministry, in any form whatsoever. This is an unbiblical, man-made, self-righteous idea, and here is why. If restoration is never permitted in leadership, then Samson should have died in the Philistine grinding house as an ex-hero slave chained to a grinding mill. Yet he cried out to God, "Remember me," and the Lord restored his strength to slay three thousand Philistine enemies. Generations later, Samson is listed in Hebrews 11:32-33 as a hero of the faith, all because of God's restoration power.

If God refused to restore David, the king should have been permanently expelled from his kingly position, sent into exile in the wilderness, and never been permitted to rule Israel. Portions of the Psalms were written when David was in great mental and spiritual agony. He could not sleep, he wept until his tears dried up, and he cried out to God for forgiveness and mercy. He lost four of his sons, but hundreds of years after David's death, God spoke to the prophets of the "sure mercies of David" (Isa. 55:3). In Psalm 136, David understood the mercy of God, because twenty-six times he wrote that God's mercy endures forever!

In Galatians 6:1, Paul wrote, *"Brethren, if a man is overtaken in any trespass, you who are spiritual restore such a one in a spirit of gentleness, considering yourself lest you also be tempted."* The word *restore* refers to "thoroughly repairing something; making it complete again." The word *fault* alludes to either a willful or an unintentional deviation from the right path.

Some are teaching that once we repent, all future sins are automatically forgiven, meaning it is never necessary to repent again. If this were true, why did Christ rebuke five of the seven churches in Revelation chapters 2 and 3, warning them of the dangers of not repenting of their sins and shortcomings? He told five churches to *repent*, which means to turn away from their present harmful, spiritual conditions and change their behavior (Rev. 2:5, 2:16, 2:22, 3:3, 3:19).

It is disturbing to observe Christians who mock and criticize another person's restoration, refusing to accept that restoration is possible or claiming it is undeserved. In situations of which I'm personally aware, those who belittle another person's restoration have an embarrassingly sinful past that they hide and make sure nobody uncovers. They desire forgiveness and restoration for themselves, and they want to make sure people never know of the terrible things they have done.

At the same time, they point the finger at other people who have done far less, as they want those people to never be restored and to suffer, in some form, for the rest of their lives. They believe that, if God does not harshly judge those individuals and cast them aside, then God isn't doing His job, and they must assist Him. Such people will even abuse scripture to appoint themselves judge and jury, as they forge a customized sword of vicious words to slice their target into pieces (Psa. 64:3).

One man was asked what he believed should happen to a minister he claimed had offended him. His answer was that he wanted the minister to lose everything and never preach again. Yet, the offended man would be enraged if people became aware of his own sinful and illegal actions that would cost him prison time if ever prosecuted.

Such action is reminiscent of the parable in Matthew 18:21-35 that speaks of forgiveness and the unmerciful servant. The kingdom of heaven is like a king who wanted to settle accounts with his servants. One man owed ten thousand talents, with one talent being equal to three thousand shekels. Some suggest that one talent was worth more than fifteen years' wages of a laborer. It was an amount the man could not repay, so this would require that the man, his wife, his children, and all that he owed be sold to help repay the debt. In other words, the man and his family would own nothing and be sold into slavery. The man pleaded with the king for more time to repay the debt, and the king showed compassion and mercy, forgiving the man of the entire debt.

But what did the forgiven man do after being forgiven? He was so ungrateful that he went out and found one of his own fellow servants who owed him a hundred pence (or denarii). This coin was a typical day's wage for an ordinary laborer. The forgiven man grabbed his servant by the throat and ordered him to pay what he owed. The servant pleaded for more time. Instead of showing the same compassion and mercy he himself had received, the forgiven man threw the servant into prison.

This greatly distressed his fellow servants, so they told their master what the man had done. Matthew 18:32-33 says that the master called for the forgiven servant and said, "You wicked servant! I forgave you all that debt because you begged me. Should you not also have had compassion on your fellow servant, just as I had pity on you?"

His master delivered him to the tormentors (torturers) until he repaid all that was due (Matt. 18:34). Tormentors were prison guards who scourged a debtor with whips until he agreed to pay back the debt, or until friends were moved with compassion and paid the debt on his behalf. In Roman times, fifteen-pound chains were placed on the debtor, and creditors were allowed to limit food until the debtor was almost starved into submission.

In verse 35, Jesus issued a stern warning, *"So My heavenly Father also will do to you if each of you, from his heart, does not forgive his brother his trespasses."* It is to our benefit to show the same mercy and compassion to other people that God has shown to us. If we do not, we eventually will suffer the consequences. Operating in unforgiveness means that you forsake your own mercy. Consistent unforgiveness will lead to a root of bitterness, and bitterness will defile your spirit. Eventually a tormenting spirit attaches to your mind. I have known of people whose bitterness placed them in such a mental bondage that they became tormented and obsessed, and they were unable to stop attacking other people.

Christ reminded His followers of the following:

> *"For with what judgment you judge, you will be judged; and with the measure you use, it will be measured back to you. And why do you look at the speck in your brother's eye, but do not consider the plank in your own eye? Or how can you say to your brother, 'Let me remove the speck from your eye,' and look, a plank is in your own eye? Hypocrite! First remove the plank from your own eye, and then you will see clearly to remove the speck from your brother's eye."*
>
> – MATTHEW 7:2-5 (NKJV)

THE RESTORATION PROCESS

For a restoration to occur, the person who has erred or sinned must acknowledge that fact and be willing to change any wrong behavior.

Second, the person must be humble before God, and with sincerity and humility, ask God and others for forgiveness. Third, if necessary, they should seek spiritual counsel to help deal with the root cause of their problem. Fourth, the person must spend much time with God in prayer and not re-enter leadership until spiritual and emotional healing has taken place. They must receive God's forgiveness and forgive those whom they need to forgive, even those involved who have not been held accountable for their own trespasses or involvement.

When a person passes through this process, they often become more sensitive to the life challenges that other people face. Oftentimes, they have more sympathy, compassion, and desire to help others in need. They can help other people learn to identify and avoid traps and ambushes. With God's help, as people correctly deal with issues, their own families and relationships can be restored and strengthened.

THE SHALAM FACTOR

The word of the Lord came to the prophet Joel about the series of destructive events that had impacted ancient Israel and the Jews, causing severe drought, starvation, and economic and agricultural suffering. God promised that if His people returned to Him with fasting, weeping, and mourning, He would restore to them the years that adversity had destroyed (Joel 1-2). In Joel 2:25, the Hebrew word for restore is *shalam*—a word that means "to make amends; to finish, to make good, to repay." The Lord indicated that He will pay back (recompense) what the enemy has seized during the tests, trials, and tribulations.

Sampson is one of the biblical examples of God's ability to repay. Sampson slew a thousand Philistines with the jawbone of a donkey (Judges 15:15), but his desire for Philistine women eventually cost him his eyesight, his physical freedom, and his anointing. For about a year he was chained to a Philistine grinding mill. Once he restored his covenant with God, he took out three thousand Philistines and died with them. But he died restored with God (Judges 16:27-30). *His end was greater than his beginning.*

When God restores, it is possible for the individuals to be restored stronger than before. Not only have valuable lessons been learned, but the ones restored have fresh trust in the faithfulness of God, a renewed mind, and a restored spirit that God can speak into. Much can be learned from those who have lived through the fire and come forth as pure gold (1 Peter 1:7).

You must continually remind yourself that your battle is not against people, but against evil, foul, or unclean spirits that are using people as their puppets. Jesus understood this when Peter rebuked Christ and told Him that He would not suffer. Instead of rebuking Peter, Jesus rebuked Satan, the true source of the wrong thoughts. Satan uses people, and people yield to wrong spirits.

When a person repents, turns from disobedience, and follows the Lord, it is our responsibility to forgive and assist in restoration. Just remember, if you choose to become hateful toward a fallen brother or sister, you may one day need the very restoration you are withholding from them.

CHAPTER 8

THE TWELVE-YEAR CYCLE OF THE DARK ANGEL

S omething astonishing was revealed to me that made so much sense and explained how demonic entities return during specific seasons. It was Christ who warned that when an unclean spirit comes out of a person, it will wander through dry places, making plans to return and linking up with seven other spirits more wicked than the first (Luke 11:26). The idea of an unclean or evil spirit returning was also evident when Christ cast out a spirit from a child who was experiencing seizures. Christ demanded that this spirit come out of the child and "enter no more into him" (Mark 9:25).

When Christ was thirty years of age, Satan tempted Him while He was in the Judean wilderness for forty days. Satan ended the temptation, but he "departed (from Jesus) for a season" (Luke 4:13). This word *season* alludes to a future appointed time.

WHEN SATAN RETURNS

Both Luke 4 and Matthew 4 record the conversation between Christ and Satan, including the temptation itself and the reaction of Christ.

The Temptation:

- *Hunger:* If you are God's Son, command the stone to become bread.

- *Jump down:* If you are God's Son, jump down from the pinnacle of the temple and the angels will watch over you.

- *Worship and kingship:* I'll give you the kingdoms of the world if you will worship me.

During the first temptation, Satan himself was the lone tempter. Forty-two months later, Satan used people at the crucifixion scene to attack Jesus for saying He is the Son of God and demand that He prove it.

The Scene at the Crucifixion:

- *Thirst:* Christ was thirsty, yet refused to drink the mixture offered Him.

- *Come down:* A thief demanded that Christ come off the cross and save Himself.

- *Kingship:* The inscription above the cross read, "King of the Jews."

The lesson to learn from the temptation of Christ is that, if a person fails to yield to a satanic temptation in one season, the adversary will back off, regroup, and return at a later point in the person's life. This explains, for example, why a person who has experienced a restoration in their marriage can encounter an unforeseen wave of attack against the marriage covenant years later. Divorces are said to occur with the greatest frequency during the first two years and during the fifth through eighth years of marriage.

A similar problem is found with substance abuse. Drug abuse relapses are as high as fifty to eighty percent within the first year. With many addictions, the reward center of the brain must be reprogrammed, or else the person finds themselves in a repetitive cycle of craving the dopamine hit. A counterattack may unfold months or years after an initial deliverance. These repetitive cycles remind me of Peter's word, *"Beloved, think it not strange concerning the fiery trial which is to try you, as though some strange thing happened unto you"* (1 Pet. 4:12 KJV).

THE REVELATION OF THE DARK ANGELS

Satan's kingdom is referred to as the kingdom of darkness, and his activities are called *works of darkness* (Rom. 13:12). We are instructed to have no fellowship with the unfruitful works of darkness (Eph. 5:11) Satan's realm of spirit rulers include *rulers of the darkness of this world* (Eph. 6:12). These dark rulers blind the minds and understanding of humanity, which keeps a person void of spiritual light that would expose the culprit behind certain activities. They work in the cloak of darkness so that they go undetected as the true source of the struggle.

A great insight for me personally came through a phone conversation. I felt impressed to contact a ministry friend who serves as the driver to a noted minister from Bogota, Colombia. Pastors have told me that this minister has a wonderful gift from the Lord and operates strongly in the word of knowledge. He is on the level of anointed men we read about in the Bible.

I had many questions and was troubled in my spirit about several things, including the death of a loved one. This minister has never met me, and the questions I had were things from my heart that only God knew the answer to. I was stunned as he knew the names of people and specific circumstances that were impossible for him to know without direct insight from the Holy Spirit.

The Spirit of the Lord gave him a revelation about my life and ministry that I was not aware of and had never heard before. Throughout periods in my life, I have sensed and even seen some type of spirit that has hindered me personally, harmed my family, or slowed down the progress of ministry assignments. This prophetic minister told me, "About every twelve years of your life, Satan sends a dark angel to attack you in some manner. He returns in twelve-year seasons…" My immediate thought was that this spirit is connected to the same spirit I have discerned at times that creates trouble, trials, and hindrances.

RESEARCHERS DISCOVERED TWELVE YEAR CYCLES

Weeks later, while researching this, I learned that some researchers involved in the field of psychology have expressed a theory that important life events seem to happen in twelve-year cycles. For example, twenty-four is the average age when a person has selected their career. Move forward to ages thirty-six, then forty-eight, then sixty, and these are ages when major events seem to transpire in a person's life. Some note that, among world leaders, the above ages were the times they made their greatest advancements, made an important discovery, or had a life changing experience.

In John 11:9 Christ said, "Are there not twelve hours in the day?" There actually are twenty-four hours in a day, but in the ancient Roman period, people were up at sunrise working outdoors, and their workday continued until the sun was setting. This would give them twelve hours of daytime to work, and twelve hours of evening to go home, eat, sleep, and repeat the cycle the next day.

After I heard the revelation from this minister, I sat down for several days and typed out a personal life review, beginning with the date I was born and moving forward marking every twelve years. Some kind of trial, test, battle, or event had occurred at or near that twelve-year timeframe.

THE DEMONIC DARK ANGEL

Between ages eleven and twelve was when two other boys and I came across the bag of pornographic magazines in the woods behind our house. That early demonic assault to corrupt my young mind was broken by an encounter with the Holy Spirit at a youth camp.

My daughter saw pornography on an electronic device at the same age, and it grew into an addiction. This cycle was also broken at a youth event (Warrior-Fest) when she was fifteen. The battle began on the same cycle as mine, about *twelve years* after her birth. In both cases, the power of the Holy Spirit at a youth event broke the yoke.

Moving forward another twelve years to age twenty-four, I experienced intense warfare that peaked at that time but had begun a couple years earlier. This was so intense that years later, I wrote a book about it titled, *Dealing with Hindering Spirits*. A group of regional drug dealers determined to close a great revival where many high school young people were being converted to Christ. The local drug dealers were losing students who sold their drugs in the county schools and local colleges.

A group of these men plotted a strategy to get the revival shut down and thereby stop disruption of their drug distribution system. Their plan included a plant within the church—a backslidden man whose job was to spread misinformation and lies, which led to an internal conflict within the church that succeeded in shutting down the revival.

During the second week of this same revival, while staying in the evangelist's apartment in the back of the church, at about three o'clock in the morning, a demonic spirit entered the apartment through the locked door. A decade later, I learned that this spirit was the "invisible agent" behind creating all the negative circumstances.

The effect of this bizarre attack lasted several years, until about 1984, when God broke through and we started preaching revivals that continued for weeks at a time. Hundreds of men and women were saved and brought into the kingdom of God. People could see the *fruit* of the ministry, which cancelled the *criticisms* against the ministry.

During the twelve-year cycles in my life, my son dealt with a lengthy addiction and could have died on at least one occasion. For several years, Pam and I felt we were in a battle of life and death for our son.

One of the strongest personal attacks that felt like an ambush was being secretly planned in November 2019. It involved a three-fold cord assault—physical, mental, and spiritual. It was an assault not only against me, but against some of my family and ministry team.

Looking back now, I see that the early pre-teen attack was a demonic attempt to bring me into bondage. The next attack in my twenties was to hinder the spiritual results of extended revivals. Later in life, the purpose was to distract me from my focus and try to get me to give up, retire, and burn out with ministry and people.

CONFIRMATION IN A DREAM

The period of 1995 to 1996 also fits into this twelve-year cycle. While flipping through my dad's books, I found a handwritten note where he penned a strange warning dream he had that was dated Monday, November 13, 1995. The note read:

> *"I saw Perry standing on the right side of two principalities or ruling powers. I saw a large one, like a man in appearance, severely rebuking and railing on the other (demonic) principality standing next to Perry. The one being rebuked seemed fearful*

of what was said to him. The greater ruling power was saying to the lesser, 'Why did you let him do it? I ordered you to block him from securing that knowledge about us. Why didn't you stop him from getting that information?'

"The one being rebuked looked fearfully at the one speaking and said, 'I tried. I don't know how he got past me. I did everything I could to stop him. I don't know how he got the information about us.'

"In anger, the larger principality shot his hands out toward the lesser principality and pulled some kind of power out of the lesser one and into his own hands. The (lesser) demonic power was pleading with him not to do it. I saw a strange dark power leave him. He was not as strong after that as he was before this happened.

"Perry had some knowledge of principalities and their power that greatly upset and agitated the greater principality. I heard him say: 'If he uses this knowledge against us, I will kill him myself.' I knew that Perry would have to be on guard against this attack."

When I read this, I recalled where Paul wrote that a messenger (literally an angel) of Satan had been assigned to hinder Paul, due to the abundance of the revelations this apostle was receiving, writing, and preaching that was shaking Satan's kingdom.

I thought back to June of 1990 when I was preaching in Romania. Two older, godly Romanian women who were in two separate cities where we preached saw a similar warning vision. Each revealed that a strong demonic prince spirit was angry at me because I was preaching something that exposed their agenda and had shaken their stronghold. They said that this prince spirit was planning to attack me and shut my mouth. It was akin to a warning I saw in a vision three years earlier.

In Dad's dream the stronger spirit was angry because of the revelation (including prophetic insight) that God was giving me and I was publicly preaching. The kingdom of darkness knows that one *divine revelation from God* can change your whole situation!

In 1994, I was with Marcus Lamb at the new Daystar studio in Dallas, preparing to minister on a topic I wrote a book about called *Unleashing the Beast.* I was reviewing notes at a large table in the studio. I stood up to stretch, and when I did, a metal light frame came loose and the entire thing crashed down on the table where my head had been. Had I not stood when I did, I would have been severely injured. That same night, with no storms in the area, the power in the studio went out, and there we sat in darkness. Someone (or something) had walked into the power room and shut off all power. Yet, no human had gone into the room. Some demonic force had set a plan in array to prevent this prophetic message from being released.

Despite all the satanic efforts to stop the release of this message, eventually it did go out and around the world.

PROPHECY FROM AN EVIL SPIRIT

I had returned from an Israel tour in November when I received a call from a minister in town, a former pastor of a large church who had become addicted to a drug and was, at the time, contemplating suicide. I went to his apartment and tried to minister to him, but he was under the control of a strong evil spirit. During my conversation, this evil spirit spoke through him saying, "I will come after *you* when you are the age he was when I attacked him!" This man had suffered from depression, and years earlier his own father, a pastor, may have taken his own life. This minister eventually received help, overcame the addiction, and began to help others dealing with addictions.

A few years passed, and I found myself experiencing strong

depression that I was not able to overcome. It lasted several months. I was between the age of thirty-five and thirty-six when this happened. The timing would have made this the third twelve-year cycle from my birth, and the same age of this minister when the enemy attacked him with an addiction. I came through this season by exposing the attack and having people pray against this spirit's strategy. It came suddenly and departed suddenly, in the month of August.

THE MONTH OF NOVEMBER

When I found Dad's note and remembered the event at Daystar and at the former minister's apartment, I decided to review the month of November. It was November of 1981 when an ambush was initiated by that demonic spirit that I saw come into the evangelist's apartment at the church in Virginia. The automobile accident my parents had in the 1960s occurred in November. I had been standing up in the front seat, and Dad made me sit down moments before the accident occurred. Had I been standing at the time of the accident, I very likely would have been thrown into the front windshield.

On my phone is a picture dated November 13, 2023 (the same day in November of Dad's dream) of my cousins and me searching through Aunt Millie's possessions at her house in Parsons. We drove from Elkins to Parsons on the same road where my family's car accident occurred in the 1960s. I had the sense that I should drive carefully across the mountain roads between the two towns, especially after dark because of all the deer. We drove the road to Parsons and back several times. I had a strange feeling when I was on that road, and I had foreboding thoughts of that accident, even though I was only a toddler when it happened.

I discussed with my cousins a plan to return the end of May and spend a few more days going through Aunt Millie's belongings. My cousin Louanna had planned a big Bava family reunion in June and suggested that I skip the end of May and wait until June when Pam could come as well for the reunion. The week I had originally planned to come, Louanna was killed in a car accident just outside of Elkins. It is possible I would have been in the car as well, had plans not changed.

WHY DO SPIRITS MOVE IN SEASONS AND CYCLES?

The Bible teaches that it is possible for a person to be possessed by an evil, foul, or unclean spirit. These spirits are called demons ("devils" in the King James – see Matthew 4:24, for example). The word in Greek is *daimonizomai* and it means "to be demon-possessed; to be possessed by a devil; to be vexed with a devil."

The Greeks considered a demon a "lesser god" in the spirit world. In Luke 11:24-26, Christ taught that an unclean spirit could enter a person, leave, and after a season of walking through dry places, return to possess the person again, bringing along seven more spirits more wicked than himself.

When Christ lived on earth in the first century AD, it is estimated the earth's population was three hundred million. There are over eight billion people on the earth today. The earth's population increases as people "multiply on the earth" (Gen 6:1). The spirit realm of heavenly angels and demons is different, though. God created a certain number of angels in the very beginning, and that number does not grow. Angels don't birth more angels.

All these angels were present when the earth was being created (see Job 38:4-7). Revelation 12:4 tells us that a third of the angelic host of heaven were expelled with Satan. With a third of the original angels having been kicked from heaven, that means there are presently two angels on God's side for every one fallen angel in Satan's kingdom.

As the earth's population increases and the angelic population of both the heavenly and satanic realms stays the same, think about what this means for the demonic realm. Two thousand years ago, they had only three hundred million people to harass and influence; now they have eight billion.

This could help explain why a dark angel or a familiar spirit is forced to move in cycles. They stay with one family for a while, become familiar with them, and create havoc. Then off they go to harass and influence some other person and family. But the time will come when they return to a previous family and try to possess, oppress, vex, and influence them again, just as Satan departed from Christ *for a season* (Luke 4:13).

One evil or unclean spirit can attach itself to a family and become familiar with the linage for many generations. While some people are indeed possessed by an evil spirit, a familiar spirit comes and goes at will. It attacks the family, departs for another assignment, and returns to that family to attack again in the future.

When Satan departed from Christ for a season (Luke 4:13), notice that the adversary failed at his three attempts, then stepped aside and waited for a better opportunity. The Apostle Paul dealt with a hindering spirit that would cause him to be harassed, arrested, beaten, or run out of town. Yet, there were times when he experienced seasons of reprieve, especially while he was in Rome, before Nero set fire to Circus Maximus.

God allows a righteous believer seasons of refreshing and relief from these spirits that harass and hinder. He will also extend grace during the times of these conflicts (2 Cor. 12:9).

Your personal or family battles might reoccur at a set time every year or every so many years. It could be a generational cycle, returning at some point to attack the next generation. Moses warned that the sins of the fathers can be passed to the third and fourth generation of those who hate the Lord (Exod. 20:5). This could be why problems such as sexual immorality, physical abuse, alcoholism, addictions, and other such troubles seem to move from generation to generation, as though being passed down in the family DNA. In fact, it could be a spirit that returns to attack the family members who are most vulnerable, either spiritually, mentally, or emotionally.

Spirits also wait for the targeted individual to open a door, which can include doors such as hidden sin, filthiness of the flesh and spirit, rebellion, disobedience, unforgiveness, and the list goes on. This causes cracks in a person's hedge of protection. Ecclesiastes 10:8 warns that whoever breaks through a hedge will be bitten by a serpent.

When Cain's countenance changed toward his brother Abel's sacrifice, God warned Cain that sin was creeping toward his door. God knew that Cain was about to open a door by committing murder, and this act would horribly impact his future (Gen. 4:7-8). Cain's sin altered his family linage for seven generations, introducing polygamy and murder (Gen. 4:23).

FAMILY CHARACTER FLAWS AND VICES

It is possible for a family to have a weakness or character flaw that passes from generation to generation. For example, in the Abrahamic linage, there was one repetitive character flaw. The patriarchs tended to tell an occasional lie or enact a deception out of fear or a desire to cover a sin. Out of fear, Abraham told the king of Egypt and King Abimelech that Sarah was his sister, instead of admitting she was his wife (Gen. 12:13; 20:2). Abraham's son, Isaac, the second generation, experienced a similar fear when he lied about Rebekah being his sister and not his wife (Gen. 26:7). Jacob, the third-generation patriarch, was told a lie by his eleven sons, all of whom conspired to tell Jacob that their youngest brother Joseph was dead, having been consumed by a wild beast (Gen. 37:32-33). All three lies were eventually exposed, bringing great embarrassment and shame.

An example of a murderous spirit gripping a family for generations is recorded in the New Testament among the four different Herods. These four were related in some way. All four were political leaders under Roman authority. All four had dealings with righteous men whom they persecuted, mistreated, or slew.

In Matthew 2:16, the first Herod, named Herod the Great, decreed that all children under two years of age be slain in and around Bethlehem. In Matthew 14:6-10, the second Herod, called Herod Antipas, gave an order for John the Baptist to be beheaded, and his head brought to him on a silver platter. Herod Agrippa I arrested James and Peter, beheaded James (Acts 12:2,) and intended to kill Peter after Passover. The fourth, Herod Agrippa II, was confronted by Paul, who preached and asked him to repent and believe on Christ. This Herod knew the stories and strange deaths of the other three men, yet he replied to Paul, "You almost persuade me to become a Christian" (Acts 26:28). This fourth Herod could have changed the future of his descendants by repenting. However, his "almost" caused him to fall short.

Other family weaknesses are evident in the linage of David. He had a total of eight wives, many whom he married before becoming king. He had eighteen children. Amnon, David's firstborn son, raped his half-sister, Tamar (2 Sam. 13). David's son Solomon carried womanizing to the extreme with three hundred concubines and seven hundred wives and princesses (1 Kings 11:3).

Always remember that, in any war, the enemy will try to get the upper hand by taking advantage of the opponents' weak spots. During the American revolution, the Red Coats (British) would form long lines on a battlefield, load their muskets, then fire. The men on the front line knew they would die first. This face-to-face method was considered "dying with honor." Later, taking a lesson from the native Indian tribes, the American fighters learned to use trees, rocks, and the woods to conceal themselves and ambush an unsuspecting British army.

When Andrew Jackson fought the battle of New Orleans, he acquired a team of sharpshooters from the mountains who were great hunters and skilled at hitting targets from long distances. An order was given that the British did not expect: Take out the officers. Suddenly, British officers were shot off their horses, sending British troops into disarray. Their officers were dying and there was nobody giving them fighting orders.

In a similar manner, removing officers and spiritual leaders has always been one of Satan's priorities. This group of people are at the top of his hit list. When the shepherds scatter, so do the sheep. Christ's death disrupted the disciples who ran in fear and hid (John 20:19). Paul's persecution caused his colleagues, such as Demas, to forsake him (2 Tim. 4:10).

Satanic attacks are strategically planned and spaced over time. While many of the challenges we deal with can be classified under the category of, "it's not the devil, it's you," we have biblical proof that there are seasons of testing caused by the return of dark angels.

CHAPTER 9

THE TWELVE-YEAR DEATH ANGEL SEQUENCES

As I continued to map out my personal and family history after receiving an unusual word from a prophet and man of God, I made a startling discovery. Not only was there a twelve-year pattern in my own life and ministry, I also found a twelve-year sequence in the deaths of my own family members and relatives on the Bava side of the family. This is the side with the Italian lineage. Our early family history, at least as far back as it began in America, started when Pete Bava immigrated from Italy to America in 1906, at the age of thirteen.

I remember my cousin telling me about an unusual incident involving her mother, my Aunt Norma Bava, that occurred while Norma was on her deathbed. Louanna was with her mother, who was a solid and dedicated Christian, at the time of her death. Before passing away, Norma had a vision of her husband in heaven, sitting on a bench with several of his buddies he had worked with in the coal mines who had also passed away. But there was something Louanna didn't understand. Just before her mom passed away, Louanna described seeing a dark angel who was watching from the corner of the room. This was confirmed by her sister, Connie. Norma was not afraid of the dark angel she was seeing and felt peace from God.

I had heard of other people who described seeing a similar dark angel, and they identified it as the angel of death. When a believer dies, God sends one or more angels from heaven to collect the soul and spirit of the one who has passed. Death is God's enemy, and it is the last enemy Christ will destroy (1 Cor. 15:26).

When the minister told me about the twelve-year cycle and a dark angel, I recalled this family story. Louanna had shared with me a very negative and troubling experience she went through beginning at age fourteen. About twelve years later, she was engaged to be married, but her fiancé, Chris, suddenly developed pneumonia and died in the hospital. Weeks before, Louanna's dad dreamt that he heard one of his daughters wailing and crying. It turned out the dream was about his youngest daughter, Louanna.

OUR ANCESTORS AND THE BLACK HANDS

At some point in my ancestral lineage, a door must have been opened that allowed a spirit occasional access to members of the family. I might have identified that door while my cousins and I were rummaging through Aunt Millie's belongings and sharing family stories. This, along with the word of knowledge from the minister, set me out to conduct family research.

It's possible the door could be linked to an early Italian group that organized in New York City after immigrants arrived. The racket then made its way to cities and rural towns in other states where Italian immigrants had settled, including West Virginia. This group was called *La Mano Nera*, or the *Black Hands*. The term Black Hands came from the act of a member sending a threatening letter and inking a black hand and a dagger at the bottom of the page. A warning from a Black Hand member could also involve leaving a bloody or coal dust dipped handprint on the windowpane of a business or home. The Black Hands attacked other Italian immigrants, especially those who had gained a measure of economic success in their new country, usually from a business or store they had opened.

The roots of this group seemingly originated in Italy in the 1700s, and it operated in the United States from around 1880 to 1920. Members were involved in extortion, kidnapping, ransom, dynamiting buildings, murder, and other nefarious deeds.

Great-grandad Pete Bava was born in 1893 in Caulonia, Italy in the Calabria region, located in the "toe of the boot." He was thirteen years old when he immigrated to the United States through Ellis Island, and his immigration papers show him asking for citizenship in 1910. By the turn of the 20th century, over four million Italians had arrived in America, most settling in port cities. Coal mining was booming in West Virginia, and by 1917, thirty percent or more of West Virginia's immigrants were Italian.

Great-granddad Pete's first son and my uncle, Joe Bava, told one of his sons that Pete was once part of the Black Hands after he arrived from Italy. That was the first I had ever heard of this organization or the fact that my great-grandfather was a member. An article about the organization was printed in a West Virginia magazine, which included a picture of local members who had been arrested in Fairmont, West Virginia. My great-grandfather, a young man at the time, was among them. It did not say why they were arrested, but it might have involved moonshine.

Prohibition, which banned the production, transportation, and sale of alcoholic beverages, began in 1920. Even before and after prohibition, the production of moonshine was common in some parts of the country. Pete and his Italian friends found a location in the hills near Pierce, West Virginia called "the rock," where they gathered to drink and produce moonshine. My granddad, John Bava, once told me of a hay wagon the men used to hide the illegal brew. In this book I relate the sad story of two of Pete's young sons, Tony and Daniel, who died at a young age because of that moonshine.

There are certainly demonic spirits connected to these types of nefarious activities and organizations. Anybody who gets involved in an organization with nefarious intent, or an illegal operation such as drug dealing, or a secret society that requires the taking of an oath, or that forbids the oath taker from revealing the organization's secrets, is opening a door for demonic spirits to attack them and their descendants. This is something that must be repented of and broken by someone in the family bloodline. Once you become aware of it, a believer can break the demonic influence that it has over the family.

Most Italians who came to America were strong Roman Catholics who attended mass. Not all Italian immigrants were involved in criminal activity. However, those who *were* involved in these Mafia-style organizations caused enough panic and turmoil that citizens and government leaders were calling for an end to Italian immigration at the turn of the 20th century.

A few Italians did not consider themselves religious, and they avoided attending mass because they witnessed certain immoral activities happening among the priests in Italy. Great-granddad Pete was one of the Italians who had nothing kind to say about the church, at least until he was healed from his deathbed and became a born-again believer.

That gives the reader some background information and explains why I suspect that my great-grandfather's involvement with this organization might be responsible for the cycle of attacks and deaths on the Bava side of the family. I have no way of knowing what kind of oath the men might have taken, but since it was a mafia-style organization, we know there's a high likelihood that oaths and secrecy were involved.

THE STRANGE TWELVE-YEAR DEATH CYCLES

After receiving the word about attacks every twelve years, I decided to see what kinds of patterns I could find with other Bava family members. I wrote down the dates of birth for family members, going back to my great-grandparents. I wrote down dates of death for those who have died. As I looked at different dates, I was shocked to discover that deaths in our family seemed to be occurring in cycles of twelve years.

When I say cycles of twelve, I'm referring to taking a primary number, in this case, twelve, and doubling it, tripling it, and so on. Twelve doubled is twenty-four. Twelve tripled is thirty-six. Keep adding twelve or multiplying twelve by 2, 3, 4, and so on, and you arrive at the numbers 12, 24, 36, 48, 60, 72, and on.

There have been numerous twelve-year cycles of events in my life and numerous death cycles of twelve on my mother's side—the Bava family. I'll give some examples. My Uncle Joe was married twice. Alvina, his first wife, bore three children before she died from cancer in 1947. Joe remarried a lady named Norma, and she bore seven children. My cousin, Joanne, was *twelve years old*, when her mother, Alvina, passed away. Alvina also died *twelve years* after her niece and my mother, Juanita, was born.

Uncle Joe passed away on August 18, 1998. His son Joe, Jr. and daughter Dorothy died in 2022, which is twenty-four years after their dad died. That is *two cycles of twelve years.*

Joe, Jr. was also married twice. His second wife, Helen, bore a daughter named Susan who passed away August 31, 2022—also *two cycles of twelve years* from my Uncle Joe's death. Louanna, Joe Jr.'s youngest sister, was a caregiver to Helen. Louanna was taking food to Joe's widowed wife Helen when Louanna was killed in the vehicular accident in 2024.

Great-grandad Pete's firstborn son Joe was born in 1912. Pete's wife and Joe's mother, Lectie Bava, passed away in 1972. Thus, Joe's mother died sixty years, or *five cycles of twelve years*, after her son Joe was born.

Pete had a son named John Bava, who was my grandfather. Pete passed away in 1985. John passed away in 1997, or *twelve years* after his dad passed away.

My grandfather, John Bava, was born in 1913. *Nine cycles of twelve* (108 years) bring us to the year 2021. Did a death occur in the Bava family on that year? Yes. John's daughter and my mother, Juanita Stone, passed away August of 2021 in a hospital in Cleveland, Tennessee.

Mom's dad, John, went to be with the Lord on April 11, 1997. He was born April 8, 1913, which means he died eighty-four years after his birth, which is *seven cycles of twelve.*

Great-grandad Pete's third son, Daniel, was born November 15, 1914. He passed away the following year. The family was drinking in Pierce, West Virginia and Daniel was there, wrapped in a blanket. Nobody noticed that the blanket blew off, and Daniel developed pneumonia and died. I was riding in a car in 1962 when Dad rounded a curve and hit a car that was stopped. Any of us could have been killed that day, but we were miraculously spared. This occurred forty-eight years, or *four cycles of twelve*, from the year Daniel was born.

There are other twelve-year cycles in the family, and the examples could continue. But I hope I have made the point. This unusual pattern runs through the same family, all of whom are blood relatives. I don't think these twelve-year cycles of death are just a coincidence.

BIBLICAL SIGNIFICANCE OF THE NUMBER 12

The number twelve appears 187 times in the Bible. All biblical numbers have meanings that are revealed within scripture from God's perspective. Twelve is a biblical number representing government and divine order.

There are twelve stones on the high priest's breastplate (Exod.

28:15-21). The twelve sons of Jacob became twelve tribes who formed the nation of Israel (Gen. 49:28). Christ was told that God stood prepared with twelve legions of angels to interrupt His son's suffering if He chose (Matt. 26:53).

Christ selected twelve men as His disciples, and later these twelve men (omitting Judas, who was replaced) became apostolic leaders who expanded the growth of the first century church (Matt. 10:1-5). In Revelation, the New Jerusalem has twelve foundation stones, upon which are the names of Christ's twelve apostles. There are twelve angels at the twelve gates, upon which are written the names of the twelve tribes of the children of Israel (Rev. 21).

During several biblical seasons, the number twelve "fell short" to the number eleven, as twelve was occasionally assaulted throughout biblical history. When Joseph was sold as a slave, that left eleven sons of Jacob at home. In Israel's early history, the tribe of Benjamin sinned and was nearly wiped out. After the apostle Judas took his own life, eleven disciples remained until the remaining eleven appointed a new twelfth apostle, Matthias, to replace Judas (Acts 1:23-26).

THE NUMBER TWELVE AND TRANSITION

In Judaism, an important transition occurs in the devout Jewish community between ages twelve to thirteen. Families conduct a Bar-Mitzvah for their sons and Bat-Mitzvah for their daughters. This coming-of-age ceremony publicly expresses that the child is transitioning to a responsible young adult. This is the age at which the young adults become responsible for their own decisions, for their right and wrong deeds, and for following and honoring the Torah, customs, traditions, Sabbaths, and festivals. The Bible notes that Jesus was twelve when He was in the temple asking and answering questions, which is part of this transition for Jewish children (Luke 2:42-49).

The number twelve reflects two important themes. First is *order and government.* The second is *transition.* The adversary delights in attempting to counterfeit the ideas and plans of God in the earth. For the adversary, the number twelve is a number to create disorder, negative transitions, and even possible death cycles.

WHAT ABOUT THE DARK ANGEL OF DEATH?

The night before the Hebrews departed from Egypt, God instructed His people to mark the outside posts of their homes in three places with lamb's blood. An angel of death would pass by and take the life of the firstborn sons in Egypt, and the blood on the door of the Hebrews' homes would allow the death angel to pass over that home. God called this death angel "the destroyer" (Exod. 12:23). The Hebrew word here for destroyer is *shachath,* a word meaning to destroy or ruin. This angel was assigned to bring death, ruin, and destruction throughout Egypt.

I was eighteen years old the first time I read about a dark angel of death, outside of scripture. It was written in a booklet by Rev. Boyd McClaren. While pastoring in Oklahoma, one of the little girls in his church was critically ill and getting worse. The family called for Rev. Boyd to come over. He was in the hospital room when the child died. For years he had asked God to allow him to see the soul of someone when they die. In this booklet, *I Saw the Death Angel*, Rev. Boyd wrote about what he saw when the child died:

> *"All of the sudden I heard something coming from above. Two black forms came down. I looked and chills went down my back. There stood before me two angels of the devil. They had the ugliest faces I had ever seen. They were about six feet tall and looked like men except they had wings. They were black from their head to their feet. They had long black hair and feet like a human, but they didn't have any hands. They reached to take*

hold of the little girl (her soul)... All at once I heard something coming. It sounded like two great eagles coming in for a power dive. The two angels of Satan looked up and you could tell they saw something, because they became scared... All at once there fell from above two great angels of the Lord..."

The story continued as he observed the dark angels being expelled from the room. Two beautiful angels of the Lord lifted the soul and spirit of the little girl from her body, taking her to paradise in heaven (2 Cor. 12:2-4).

SEASONS OF ANGELS

Only once, in 1977, have I seen an angel of God visibly manifest before my natural eyes. It was during an evening campmeeting service at the Church of God campground in Roanoke, Virginia. The angelic image appeared to the left of the platform, then vanished within a few seconds. Honestly, it frightened me! After this I began studying the appearances and purposes of angelic assignments. John records a wonderful narrative that reveals how angels minister in specific seasons:

"Now there is at Jerusalem by the sheep market a pool, which is called in the Hebrew tongue Bethesda, having five porches. In these lay a great multitude of impotent folk, of blind, halt, withered, waiting for the moving of the water. For an angel went down at a certain season into the pool, and troubled the water: whosoever then first after the troubling of the water stepped in was made whole of whatsoever disease he had."

– JOHN 5:2-4

The Greek word for season in that passage is *kairos*, referring to a set time in the future. Angels of both God and Satan function in seasons. After forty days of temptation, Satan departed from Christ for a season, meaning the adversary would return at a set time in the future. In this case it was forty-two months later at the crucifixion. The angel at the pool of Bethesda was not present and performing miracles at the pool twenty-four hours a day. But he would arrive at set moments, and the first person who responded was healed.

Angels are rarely *seen* but their presence can be *felt*. At different times throughout my ministry, I am confident that I have encountered the presence of an heavenly angel, both in private and during anointed ministry services.

TRACKING SEASONS OF ATTACK

One would expect that most conflicts would emerge in a person's life from youth to about mid-life, then slowly fade as we get older. However, that is not necessarily the case. In scripture, there seem to be three points of intense crisis: at the *beginning* of any major assignment, in the *middle* of an important assignment, and toward the *end* of a person's life.

After Paul's conversion in Damascus, he immediately became a kill target for his enemies. He escaped over the wall in a basket, avoiding his first death attempt. In his mid-life he experienced a series of arrests and near-death escapes. At his concluding moments, he was beheaded in Rome.

When Christ was an infant, Herod assigned troops to find Him and slay Him. He escaped to Egypt for a season. In the middle of His ministry, people attempted to stone Him, but He successfully escaped. His earthly life ended at His crucifixion.

David's first battles were fighting bears and giants early in life. He fought Philistine armies as an adult—his mid-life battle. He suffered physically at the end of his life with a dreaded and painful disease (see Psalm 38).

Some have assumed that by the time you turn sixty, your only challenges are some minor physical ailments. Yet, my most intense conflict began to unfold around age sixty.

Along with tracking the twelve-year death cycles of my mother's relatives, I also began to track my own life to see if various attacks followed the same twelve-year pattern. I'm not suggesting that every problem we encounter is an attack from the enemy. Some warfare is self-invited, some is brought on by a lack of wisdom, while some warfare is undeniably a planned attack of the enemy.

As I did with my family, I started with my date of birth and tracked twelve-year cycles. A pattern emerged that was shocking at times. In charting this, an attack was not necessarily initiated on that twelve-year cycle, but the strange battle or transition had already manifested and was raging on that year. Of all the twelve-year cycles, the one marking the year 2019, just prior to the release of the covid virus, would top all others. As we entered 2020, I was hit from many directions—in body, soul and spirit.

RELEASE OF THE EVIL ANGELS

In Psalm 78, David detailed numerous events that occurred when Israel wandered forty years through the wilderness. You have heard much of this taught in Sunday School or sermons. However, perhaps you are unaware of two verses in Psalm that allude to signs that occurred in Egypt, prior to the Exodus:

> "He cast upon them the fierceness of his anger, wrath, and indignation, and trouble, by sending evil angels among them. He made a way to his anger; he spared not their soul from death, but gave their life over to the pestilence."
>
> – PSALM 78:49-50 (KJV)

The Hebrew word for angels here is *mal'ak*, which is translated as angels ten times in the King James Version of the Old Testament. It is also translated as messenger. In the Exodus narrative, there is a death angel (singular) and not death angels (plural) that manifested the night before Israel departed. In context, David was speaking of the many plagues, including the deaths of the firstborn.

We know that God will send seven angels from His Holy Temple with vials and plagues to pour out judgments upon the earth during the Great Tribulation (Rev. 8, 15, 16). It is possible that God also sent ten judgment angels to release the ten horrible plagues and pestilences against the rebellious Egyptians.

The Bible has things to say about rebellion. Proverbs 17:11 reads, *"An evil man seeks only rebellion; therefore, a cruel messenger shall be sent against him."* Pharaoh kept rebelling and thus encountered a cruel messenger, or angel.

In the Old Testament are four different Hebrew words for rebellion. Some refer to becoming an *apostate* by resisting the Spirit and turning against God (Jer. 28:16). Another verse alludes to a *revolt* against authority (Job 34:37). In other places, the word indicates a person who resists God because of their *bitterness* (Deut. 31:27). The Prophet Samuel warned Saul, *"Rebellion is as the sin of witchcraft, and stubbornness is as iniquity and idolatry"* (1 Sam. 15:23). Under Moses' law, once a witch was exposed, the sorceress was sentenced to death (Exod. 22:18). Saul's rebellion eventually opened the door for the death angel to visit the arrogant and backslidden king on a battlefield.

Saul was wounded in battle. He asked his armor bearer to end his life, but the faithful guard refused. Saul fell upon his own sword and took his own life (1 Sam. 31:4). Saul wasted thirteen years pursuing David with the intent of taking that same sword and killing the young warrior. Yet, Saul himself died by his own sword, reminding us that all who take the sword shall perish by the sword (Matt. 26:52).

SPIRITS THAT ARE MORE WICKED

Jesus spoke of a person being possessed with one spirit, who eventually became possessed with seven more spirits more wicked than the first (Luke 11:26). These seven other spirits are more evil in their intent and ability to deceive. The Spirit of the Lord departed from Saul, and an evil spirit from the Lord tormented him (1 Sam. 16:14-23). As Saul continued to despise David, the jealous king set ambushes against David, even attempting to pierce him with spears. Eventually other more wicked spirits seized possession of Saul. Here are seven types of spirits and evil inclinations that entered Saul's life:

- *Envy:* He became envious of David's popularity.

- *Conspiracy:* He believed his children had conspired against him.

- *Hatred:* He hated anyone who supported David.

- *Murder:* He slew priests who had defended David.

- *Rebellion:* He sought out a witch for spiritual advice.

- *Fear:* He became afraid that David would destroy his legacy.

- *Suicide:* He fell upon his own sword and ended his life.

I have heard people proclaim that "sin is sin, and all sins are equal." This is partially true. All sin is *sin*, but not all sins are *equal*. There are sins against *yourself*, sins against *others*, and sins against *God*.

An example of a sin against yourself would be an addiction to anything that is destroying your body, which is the temple of the Holy Spirit (1Cor. 3:17). Sins against others include covetousness, bearing false witness, slandering, or unforgiveness. Sins against God include taking His name in vain, disobeying His Word, unbelief, or blasphemy.

There are sins of ignorance and sins of knowledge. We know that all sins are not equal because, if you speak against the Son of Man, you can be forgiven. However, if you blaspheme the Holy Spirit, you cannot be forgiven, as that is the unpardonable sin (Luke 12:10).

Pulling another person into a sin that someone else is committing is a terrible kind of sin. What about drug dealers who sell illegal narcotics to people, thereby endangering the lives of the innocent and destroying families and futures? Adultery is another example of a sin that affects not just the people sinning, but their families as well. This often leads to the breakup of families and divorce, with children caught in the middle. Consider an offended individual who slanders other people, using malicious language to draw other people into their offense, thereby poisoning the spirits of others and expecting them to choose sides.

In Second Chronicles 18, God allowed a lying spirit in the mouths of four hundred prophets of Ahab to give a false prediction that Ahab would engage in a battle and return home victorious. The truth was, God had planned for Ahab to die in battle. One true prophet warned the evil king he would die, but instead Ahab listened to the chanting of four hundred slick-tongued false prophets. Ahab believed that his majority opinion was more accurate than one lone prophet who was pulled from a dungeon to give a warning message directly from God.

Evil angels and evil spirits are the masters of deception. The Apostle Paul warned of men posing as messengers of Christ but were sent by Satan, who had transformed himself into an angel of light (2 Cor. 11:13-15). When you see someone posing in the name of the Lord, yet deceiving, harming, or destroying others for their own personal agenda, this is an "angel of light" deception.

BAD DAYS ON THE CALENDAR

We all have bad days here and there throughout the year, but it usually isn't the same day every year. The Jews, however, have marked a bad day on their calendar that arrives every year at the same time. They note that, historically, this is considered the worst day in Jewish history. It is the 9th of Av. Here are some troubles in Jewish history that occurred on the 9th of Av:

- Ten of the twelve spies that Moses sent into the Promised Land brought back a negative report, causing the people to wander in the wilderness forty years.

- Babylonian armies destroyed the first Jewish Temple in 586 BC.

- Roman armies destroyed the second Jewish Temple in AD 70.

- Jewish leader Simon bar Kochba was slain at the final battle at Betar in AD 135.

- In the year 1290, England expelled Jews.

- In the year 1306, the Jews were expelled from France.

- In 1492, the Jews were removed from Spain.

- In 1914, Germany declared war on Russia, catapulting the world into World Wars I and II.

- In 1942, mass deportation of Jews to the Treblinka concentration camp began.

- In 2005, Jews were forced to abandon their homes and businesses and move out of the Gaza strip.

According to Orthodox Jewish commentaries, the 9th of Av is the saddest day of the year on the Jewish calendar and is marked as a day destined for tragedy.

Some families also can identify a specific time when it seems that difficulty rears its ugly head each year, as well as certain months when spiritual breakthroughs seem to occur. Personally, I have observed that May has had its challenges and seasons of attack. Other times it was six months later in November.

WHY DOES GOD PERMIT IT?

People often ask why God allows the dark kingdom to orchestrate attacks. What is God's perspective behind such warfare?

God permits conflict and attacks for different reasons. His purpose is to use every test, trial, or temptation to expose the true enemy and realign you into His perfect will. Sometimes this includes God removing people from your life, moving you away from the familiar, or humbling you by removing pride.

The adversary, however, assigns every assault with the primary intent to steal, kill, and destroy (John 10:10). When he can't kill you, he hopes, at the very least, to weaken your faith and cause distractions that hinder your dreams, desires, and plans.

God never wastes a test or a trial. Sometimes the tests and trials include a season of purification, also known as the *gold* test:

> *"That the genuineness of your faith, being much more precious than gold that perishes, though it is tested by fire, may be found to praise, honor, and glory at the revelation of Jesus Christ..."*
>
> – 1 PETER 1:7 (NKJV)

Before gold can be molded and formed into a valuable golden vessel, impurities imbedded in the gold nuggets are removed by firing it at an extremely high temperature. This melts the gold and brings impurities to the surface so they can be removed. After the purity is determined, the gold is cast or molded into whatever valuable object the artisan intends.

Peter knew of what he spoke when he wrote that verse. His name had been Simon bar Jonah, but Jesus changed his name to Peter, which means rock or stone. However, this future rock was rough around the edges, and he required a season of sifting, which God permitted so that he could be crushed and come forth as a more refined vessel.

The dark angel, prince spirits, or demonic entities will return at a more opportune time. They can initiate a test but cannot control the outcome. The conclusion of the test is based on the timing of the Lord, your ability to endure, and your determination to remain standing.

CHAPTER 10

THE WAR IS ON—ANGELS OF LIGHT AND DARKNESS

Throughout the Bible, angels play a role that extends from creation, all the way to the time that the New Jerusalem arrives on the New Earth (Rev. 21). When the angels of God were seen, there were common characteristics noted in the Bible. These include:

- They were wearing white garments (Matt. 28:3; John 20:12; Acts 1:10)

- Sometimes the garments are called linen (Ezek. 9:2, 10:6; Dan. 10:5, 12:6, 7)

- They appear bright or in light (Ezek. 1:4-5, 27-28; Acts 12:7)

- They show up to battle the kingdom of darkness (Dan. 10; Rev. 12:7-10).

There are levels of authority among both God's heavenly angels and demonic dark angels. God's highest-ranking angel is Michael, the archangel. Michael is the angelic guardian for the nation of Israel (Daniel 12:1). He also is the chief angel that confronts Satan face to face. After Moses' death, Michael wrestled Satan for the body of Moses, which was eventually buried in an undisclosed location, in a valley in Jordan, by God Himself (Jude 9, Deut. 34:5-6). During the Great Tribulation, Michael and his angels will war against Satan and his angels, expelling them from the cosmic heavens to earth (Rev. 12:7-9).

The ministry of holy angels is necessary to battle demonic dark angels or principality spirits. The highest angels in the satanic kingdom are principalities (Eph. 6:12). These prince spirits are given authority over cities, nations, and prophetic empires.

Two biblically noted dark prince angels are called the prince of the kingdom of Greece and the prince of Persia (Dan. 10:13, 20). For over two hundred years, from 538 to 333 BC, the prince of Persia oversaw political events involving the Persian empire. After the Greeks over-threw the Persians, this second prince spirit worked behind the scenes during the Grecian Empire's rule, from 333 to 63 BC, which concluded with the rise of the Roman Empire.

The prophet Daniel, from the time of his exile to his death, lived in Babylon about seventy years. Daniel survived two empires and five different kings. God assigned His special messenger angel named Gabriel to interpret Daniel's visions, and God assigned Michael the archangel to oversee the cosmic war between the angels of darkness and light.

God sends angels to become involved when there are stronger satanic powers at work. We each are to deal with our own tests, trials, and temptations through the weapons of prayer, fasting, the Word of God, and the strength of the Holy Spirit. However, when we encounter an attack from high-ranking agents of the dark kingdom, we may require the assistance of an angel of God.

Angels were present for Christ at His birth, at the conclusion of His forty-day temptation, during His agony in the Garden of Gethsemane, after His resurrection, and at His ascension on the Mount of Olives. The reasons were to give Him revelation, to strengthen Him during his lowest moments, and to bring warnings or important announcements.

I NEEDED ANGELIC ASSISTANCE

Years ago, I experienced a strange vision where I was in a building with double glass doors. I saw my large travel suitcase and my ministry briefcase, both of which have wheels attached. In the dream, both the suitcase and briefcase raised off the floor, as though an invisible hand had lifted them by the handles. Both were being moved away from me as they began to slide toward the glass doors.

I yelled, "Hey, come back here! Those are mine. Leave them alone!" It was as though an invisible spiritual hindrance was planning to disrupt my evangelistic travel ministry.

Then I found myself looking down a long, narrow hallway. I saw someone whom I knew in the dream to be Satan. He is not a red creature with horns and a pitchfork, as he is sometimes portrayed in artwork; instead, he looked like a well-built, strong, and determined man. He advanced toward me, as though coming after me with the intent to do harm. I heard a voice tell me what to say and I yelled out, "Satan, get behind me in the name of Yeshua!" (Note that the voice told me to use the Hebrew name of Jesus.) He stopped momentarily as though he was uncertain what to expect. Then he continued toward me. I heard the voice tell me to call for Michael the archangel to fight Satan on my behalf. I did so, and a second time I yelled, "Satan, get behind me in the name of Yeshua!" This time he stumbled over and fell onto one knee and stopped.

I knew by revelation of the Spirit that the Lord would not permit him to fulfill his entire planned strategy, because God would interrupt it. This would require ordering him to get behind me, in the name of Yeshua, and asking God to send supernatural assistance from a warring angel.

Our human eyes are veiled to the spirit world for good reason. To see into the realm of spirits can be fearful. When Daniel saw the visions of both dark spirits and angels of God, at times the strength left his body and he found himself on the ground face down (Dan. 8:18; 10:15). When people in the Bible saw angels, they were often told to "fear not" (Gen. 21:17; Dan. 10:12).

Imagine driving your car down the highway, looking into the vehicle beside you, and seeing the evil or unclean spirits working through people in the car. Think how people would react if they could see every angel flying around vehicles to protect the families of God during their journeys. Imagine waking up in the middle of the night and seeing hooded beings or an angel glowing and lighting up the room. Except in rare cases where God removes the veil and allows someone to see these beings, rest assured He has hidden them from our view for a reason.

CALLING ON ANGELIC ASSISTANCE

The word angel or angels is found in the English translation of the Bible nearly three hundred times. Angels are also called heavenly host (Luke 2:13). Angels were not created just to guard the entrance of heaven or to remain in heaven. They are involved with God's plan for mankind on the earth. After Adam and Eve transgressed, God drove them out of the Garden and placed a cherub with a flaming sword at the east of Eden to guard the way to the tree of life (Gen. 3:24).

Decades ago, my dad saw a vision of his half-brother Morgan being killed in a terrible car wreck in West Virginia. Dad attempted to call Morgan, but he did not answer the phone. Dad immediately began to intercede and travail for Morgan to be spared.

The Lord impressed upon Dad to pray that the angel who showed up for Dad many times would be sent to protect Morgan from premature death. Dad did so, and he prayed until he felt a release. Morgan barely missed being hit head on by a coal truck that would have killed both him and his driver.

On several occasions, our family's life was spared through direct involvement with an angel. We know of specific times when our lives were spared on the highway.

We can call upon God in the day of trouble to be delivered (Psa. 50:15). Angels are given charge over us to keep (preserve) us from danger (Psa. 91:11-12). We can pray to Christ and call upon His name (John 16:23-24). To call upon is to focus your faith, prayers, and words in one direction, believing in your heart that you have been heard and God will answer.

In your lifetime, there may have been many times when angels of God were involved in your protection, direction, or inspiration, yet you were unaware of their assistance. We should thank God, not only for what we know He has done, but for things He did that we were unaware of, when angels battled on our behalf.

CHAPTER 11

CHARTING YOUR PERSONAL AND FAMILY ATTACK CYCLES

Your own family might be experiencing a negative generational pattern of some sort, whether it's twelve years or another timeframe. It is possible to chart this to see if a pattern emerges within your family and your ancestral line. Here are some interesting things I discovered within my family.

When my mother, Juanita, was thirty-nine years of age, she suffered a miscarriage. When my wife Pam was thirty-nine, she became pregnant and had a miscarriage. When my mother was forty, she gave birth to a daughter, Melanie, who is my youngest sibling. At age forty, my wife Pam gave birth to our daughter Amanda, who was born twelve years after her brother Jonathan.

My mother had a severe gallbladder attack at age twenty-one that required surgery. At age twenty-one, her son and my brother, Phillip, was struck with a sudden gallbladder attack that required emergency surgery.

In another strange pattern of events, my dad's mother, my grandmother Nalvie, experienced a nervous breakdown after her first husband was killed in a hunting accident. At the time Nalvie had three children. My wife's mother, Stella, experienced a breakdown after going through a divorce. At the time, she was thirty-nine and had three small children.

Years passed and one of Stella's daughters, who had three young children, also experienced a minor breakdown following a divorce. She was the same age as her mother when she went through a similar type of event.

Early in 2020, I collapsed in my office, so physically weak that I could not stand up. I developed symptoms that were aligned with those that a clinical therapist would call a breakdown. It has taken several years to regain strength and reprogram my thinking to deal with emotional triggers that created physical reactions and panic attacks.

DISCOVERING NUMERICAL PATTERNS

Repetitive patterns are not random, and they often align with numbers that have a significant biblical meaning. However, Satan, being the master counterfeiter, will take a spiritual number and turn its meaning into something diabolical. The following list compares several examples:

Biblical Number	God's Meaning	Satan's Counterfeit
3	unity, oneness	division, confusion
6	mankind, the human race	carnality, the flesh
7	completion, perfection	tribulation, anguish
12	government, order	disorder, division
30	spiritual maturity	spiritual dysfunction
40	completion of a battle	initiation of a battle

50	freedom, liberty, release	bondage, depression
70	completion of assignment	disrupting a good end

There are many examples of how both God and Satan view these numbers. Solomon was the third king of Israel. In his early teens, Solomon started out seeking God's wisdom. However, later in life he succumbed to his fleshly appetites. As a result, the Lord allowed three adversaries (literally "satans" in Hebrew) to be raised up against Solomon. They were Hadad, Rezon, and Jeroboam (1 Kings 11:14, 23, 26).

Adam was created on the sixth day of creation, a day that was blessed by God. Yet, when the Antichrist is unveiled, his number is linked with three sixes, or 666 (Revelation 13:18).

The high priest in the Old Testament wore a gold breastplate with twelve gemstones carved with the corresponding names of the twelve tribes of Israel. When Lucifer is identified as an anointed cherub in Ezekiel 28, we learn that he was created with a covering. But instead of twelve gems, the Bible mentions that he wore nine stones as his covering. Three stones were missing (Ezek. 28:13). As a rebellious archangel, Satan would cause division among the angels and separate one-third from God (Rev. 12:4).

Christ waited until He was thirty years of age to enter public ministry (Luke 3:23). Moses wrote that a man could enter the priesthood at age thirty (Num. 4:3). Christ waited until age thirty for public ministry so He would fulfill the law.

When Satan inspired Judas to betray Christ, Judas was rewarded with thirty pieces of silver (Matt. 27:3). For God, the number thirty represented maturity for ministry. From Satan's viewpoint, the same number became the reward for betraying innocent blood.

The number forty is unique. During Noah's flood it rained forty days and nights (Gen. 7:12). Goliath taunted the army of Israel for forty consecutive days (1 Sam. 17:16). Both Isaac and Esau were forty years of age when they each took a wife (Gen. 25:20; 26:34). Moses spent two periods of forty days on the holy mountain, fasting both times (Exod. 34:28). Israel was tested in the wilderness for forty years (Deut. 8:2).

In the New Testament, Christ was tempted by Satan for forty days (Luke 4:2). In this instance, as in other references, the number forty is associated with testing, temptation, and trials. However, after Christ was resurrected, He was seen alive for forty days (Acts 1:3). This forty-day period was a season of victory and triumph, including overcoming death and hell. On one side, we see that the number forty represents a season of testing, trial, or battle. When God flips the meaning, forty becomes a time of great overcoming and opportunity.

Each year there is a set time on the Jewish calendar called the forty days of Teshuvah. The season commemorates Moses' second trip to the top of Sinai, where he interceded to God on behalf of the children of Israel, asking that they not be destroyed. This is also where he received a second set of commandments on tablets of stone.

The forty days conclude on the Day of Atonement, a time when Jews teach that a person's fate is sealed for the following year. In Isaiah 55:6-7, the prophet told the Jewish nation to "seek the LORD while He may be found and call upon Him while He is near." Jewish sages teach that the time Isaiah spoke of, and the time when the gates of heaven are open to hear prayers, is during the ten days from Rosh Hashanah to Yom Kippur. This becomes a time for the Jewish people for repentance and a return to observance of God's commandments.

Of course, we know that God hears us every day, and we should always remain repentant and follow His commands. Teshuvah is still a time to look back and reflect upon our actions, words, and spiritual walk as we look ahead. It is a time to focus on forgiving others.

My family and I also give "seasons of God" offerings for Kingdom work during this forty-day season of Teshuva. We have been amazed to see that some of our greatest ministry breakthroughs manifested on the fortieth day, and we have heard others give the same testimony. Thus, a number that is often associated with testing and trials can become a time when God's blessings and victories are released.

TRACKING YOUR FAMILY PATTERNS

Tracking family cycles and patterns begins with discovery. First, make a genealogical list of past and present family members, including yourself, going back as far as you can on both sides of your family. Beside each name, write their date of birth and, if they have passed away, their date of death. Make note of any severe attacks, diseases, divorces, trauma, or death. Examine the dates and see if any events occurred on a cycle. Do you notice a pattern of years when something negative or positive happened? Did certain battles repeat themselves in repetitive cycles?

If a pattern emerges, this can make you aware of the possibility that a new plot, test, temptation, or other malicious activity could be being planned in the future, thus showing you the timeframe in which it could manifest. Knowing this will make you more aware, more discerning, more watchful, and more prayerful leading up to that season.

Based on my thoughts about my great-grandfather's membership in the Black Hands mafia-style organization, I suggest that you also examine your own family line to see if anybody was involved in activities that allowed the enemy an open door to attack the descendants' bloodline. Repent on behalf of your family for that involvement, break any curses and agreements that their activities brought upon the family bloodline, and close all doors that their oaths and activities opened that gave the enemy access.

TYPES OF TESTING

Biblically there are three types of testing:

- *Common* temptation, which people deal with routinely. No temptation has overtaken you, but such as is common to man (1 Cor. 10:13).

- *Seasonal* testing and temptation will repeat during certain seasons (Luke 4:13). These could repeat at an opportune time, as with the example of Jesus. Seasonal temptations can often be tracked on a cycle.

- The *hour of testing* could involve sudden death, a traumatic divorce, or any kind of situation that creates severe and long-term trauma. The hour of testing is an intense struggle that often cannot be "prayed away in advance," although God could give advance warnings about it. God permits the hour of testing, and it requires faith, patience, and endurance to make it through.

PROACTIVE OR REACTIVE

When possible, it is always best to know and be able to respond in advance before a crisis of faith is unleashed. Here are five methods the Holy Spirit uses to warn us in advance of a pre-planned strategic attack that is coming your way.

1. Discerning the Signs - Jesus told the Pharisees that they could successfully view the sunset to tell if the weather on the horizon would be clear or stormy, yet they were blind to discerning the signs of the times. Discerning the signs around you can often be detected when we "watch and pray" (Matt 26:41). One of my past weaknesses was being so busy that I became blinded by familiarity. Others close to me would observe the actions and words of certain people, but I paid little to no attention until the serpent bit. If you cannot see, but others that you trust can, pay attention to early warning signs and respond accordingly, using wisdom and discretion.

2. Spiritual Dreams - Throughout the Bible, God warned His followers of impending trouble. Sometimes He revealed secrets being plotted in the enemy's camp by giving a warning dream. The man speaking in the dream might have been an angel of the Lord. On several occasions during my dad's life, he was warned of harm and danger being planned against himself, a family member, a church member, or even the nation. Through the years, we both watched the attempted plan of the enemy emerge. However, these dreams put us on guard, and we were prepared and knew what to do in each circumstance.

3. Warnings from Spiritual Friends – Proverbs 20:18 teaches to establish plans by wise counsel and good advice: *"Every purpose is established by counsel: and with good advice make war."* David was offered Saul's armor before facing Goliath. But David rejected what he had never used in battle, and instead selected his own weapon—a slingshot and a rock. Never allow yourself to be pulled into conflict that you are not assigned to. Select your battles. Even when you feel strongly about something, instead of being led to act or speak according to the desires of your flesh, it is better to remain silent, cool off your emotions, and select your time and place for a face-to-face encounter to address the situation. Other times, it is best to walk away, forgive, and move in another direction to something new. However, when you seek counsel, never take advice from a bitter, angry, unforgiving person, as they will corrupt your spirit, just as their own is corrupted.

4. A Gut Feeling or Deep Uneasiness - Women tend to be more aware of and attentive to this uneasiness than men. A godly woman will have a gut feeling discernment that something feels wrong. I recall at least three times over the course of marriage that my wife has warned me about certain people that she felt uncomfortable with. In each case she was proven correct, and it was necessary to break off all contact with the individuals. Pam can sense things, while I am oblivious to it. When your spirit begins to feel uneasy, restless, or burdened, this means that you need to stop and pay attention. Watch and pray.

5. Be Proactive and Not Reactive – Being proactive means to anticipate and deal in advance with an expected situation or difficulty. It means acting on the potential situation before it happens, instead of waiting until it happens and reacting to it. Being proactive can help bring the positive outcome you desire, while responding after it happens can bring negative or mixed results. Remember the old Andy Griffin program, where the outspoken deputy Barney Fife dealt with problems by suggesting, "Nip it in the bud!"

God warns us to prepare us, not to scare us. On several occasions my father or I had spiritual dreams in which the biblical symbolism in the dream was interpreted as a warning of trouble ahead. Common symbols in the dreams were large snakes or other dangerous beasts. Such symbols often represent danger that will be caused by a wicked person who is after you or something you possess, or the person intends to stop something God is doing in your life. Animals that kill with their teeth, such as alligators, represent a large-mouthed enemy who will operate through verbal attacks. Serpents in a dream can represent evil words or intentions coming against you.

One of the primary problems ministers must deal with is verbal attacks that the enemy uses as he attempts to hinder whatever the minister is accomplishing for the Kingdom of God. Warnings make us more alert and more guarded, and warnings enable us to avoid or lessen the problem using God's wisdom, or to stand amid the onslaught.

The Holy Spirit is the greatest agent of God who knows and can reveal the future. The Holy Spirit will "guide you into all truth" and "show you things to come" (John 16:13). This might come through a dream or vision, a strong inner burden or a gut feeling, warnings from close friends or ministry partners, or inspiration from your own prayers. God has provided every spiritual weapon we need to destroy the works of Satan and position us as overcomers.

CHAPTER 12

RELEASING AND HEALING WOUNDS OF THE SOUL

Psalm 23 is the most recognized Psalm in the world. In verse three David wrote, "He (God) restores my soul...." When David wrote this Psalm, he was being chased throughout the Judean Wilderness by King Saul, who was attempting to assassinate the future king of Israel. David was walking through the "valley of the shadow of death," yet he understood that God, His Shepherd, was with him (Psa. 23:4). David noted that in the dry, desolate wilderness, God would provide and "prepare a table," even when David was surrounded by enemies (Psa. 23:5).

David was a man after God's own heart, a pursuer of righteousness, and a warrior who fought God's enemies. Yet, for thirteen years, from age seventeen to thirty, he lived like a fugitive on the run, camping out in caves and tents, and being guarded by six hundred mighty men. He faced and slew lions, bears, giants, Philistines, and surrounding tribes. He spent years dealing with his own father-in-law, King Saul. During this troubling season, David's wife was also given to another man. Imagine being David.

A WOUNDED SOUL

The word *soul,* found 419 times in the Bible, alludes to the life force that is within the body. At creation, Adam became a "living soul" after God breathed into his nostrils the breath of life (Gen. 2:7). The soul is the part of you that expresses feelings, emotions, and desires. The various Psalms reveal characteristics of the human soul:

- Psalm 6:3 - the soul can be *vexed* (troubled, dismayed).

- Psalm 7:2 - the soul can be *torn* to pieces, as if attacked by a lion.

- Psalm 7:5 - the soul can be *persecuted* (pursued, over-taken) by enemies.

- Psalm 13:2 - the soul can *wrestle* and feel *sorrow* deep in the heart.

- Psalm 42:5 - the soul can be *cast down* (pressed down, in despair).

- Psalm 55:18 - the soul can have *battles* set against it.

- Psalm 63:9 - people can seek a person's soul to *destroy* it.

- Psalm 88:3 - the soul can be full of *troubles.*

- Psalm 107:5 - the soul can *faint* within the body.

- Psalm 143:6 - the soul can become *spiritually thirsty.*

- Psalm 143:12 - the soul can be *afflicted* by your enemies.

Intense spiritual battles disturb your spirit, but they also impact your soul. From scripture in the Psalms alone, we see that the impact can manifest through restlessness, oppression, depression, fear, anxiety, and physical weakness. The soul also processes emotions and feelings such as hurt, pain, and grief.

BEING CAST DOWN

David asked himself the question, *"Why are you cast down, O my soul? And why are you disquieted within me?"* (Psa. 42:5). The Hebrew word *disquieted* refers to something boisterous or turbulent, something so clamorous that it completely distracts a person's soul.

The phrase *cast down* was a sheep metaphor in David's time. It alludes to a sheep rolling over on its back and being unable to get up on it four legs. It becomes helpless. If it remains in that position, it panics as its legs flail in the air. This causes gases to build up in its lungs, cutting off the animal's breathing. Without the shepherd's intervention, it will eventually die. In this physical condition, it also cannot run, making it easy prey for a predator.

David's soul was cast down, but he understood that he must not cast aside his faith in a crisis, just as we must not "roll over" and quit. The Apostle Paul describes a person who casts aside their faith as a "castaway" (1 Cor. 9:27), which refers to becoming unapproved, counterfeit, or by implication, worthless.

In contemporary interpretation, becoming cast down is when something knocks you off your feet. This could happen with the sudden loss of your job that stops all income. For some, it could be the sudden and unexpected death of a family member. Another person's moment of becoming cast down might be the medical report that says you have a life-threatening disease. Any number of situations can cause the soul to be cast down.

SIGNS THAT YOUR SOUL IS CAST DOWN

Just as with a sheep that rolls over and experiences breathing changes, a person who is cast down can experience a rapid heartbeat, a rise in blood pressure, and higher stress levels. This often leads to a range of emotions, from withdrawal and depression to outbursts of anger and thoughts of retaliation.

There are enemies from within and enemies from without. Some of David's closest friends had turned into enemies. Many of the Psalms read like a personal diary that David penned; for example, he wrote:

> *"Yea, mine own familiar friend, in whom I trusted, which did eat of my bread, hath lifted up his heel against me."*
>
> – PSALMS 41:9 (KJV)

Whoever this close friend was, he and David had fellowshipped together at the dinner table. The term "lifting up the heel" metaphorically alludes to a man attempting to feed his favorite riding horse, when suddenly the horse begins to kick up his back legs, which can cause the owner serious harm or even death.

Attacks from people we don't know or don't have a relationship with have little impact on us. There is no love lost because there is no relationship. Friendless opinions are just opinions, often coming from manipulative people with a critical spirit who hold multiple grudges and offenses, and therefore they have an ax to grind every day of their lives.

It's different when sudden attacks and betrayal come from a close friend with whom a relationship has been built over the years. Betrayal means "an act of deliberate disloyalty." People who betray friends or family exaggerate someone's personal weakness, expose private information, and tell outright lies. The betrayer often wants to enhance their position with others, especially in this day of social media and paid clickbait.

Notice that when Judas betrayed Christ, Judas also had the unmitigated gall to expose Christ and have Him arrested while at His secret place of prayer. Jesus, however, still called Judas "friend."

If you have been betrayed by someone, or if you are familiar with someone who is a betrayer, you might notice that they are eager to reveal everything they know about their former friend or family member. Yet, the betrayer makes sure their own secrets, sins, or crimes remain hidden, as they elevate themselves by bringing other people down.

Why does a friend betray? The root might seem to be a wound that the betrayer perceives they have received from the one they are betraying, but the root often goes much deeper. The perceived offense is merely an excuse to avoid dealing with a deeper problem in the betrayer's life. The individual with unhealed wounds often hides his or her own life problems by embarrassing and humiliating other people.

RELIGIOUS SOUL WOUNDS

The most difficult and often unexplainable wounds are ones that come from those who call themselves Christians, because you don't expect this behavior from Christians. Yet, remember that according to Zechariah 13:6, in the future, the Jews will ask the Messiah, "Where did you get those wounds in your hands?" Christ will answer, "In the house of my friends."

Christ came to minister to His own people, yet the religious sects dishonored and rejected Him (John 1:11). Christ called Judas "friend" at the very moment Judas was betraying him (Matt. 26:50). Painful wounds can be caused by fellow Christians, especially those whom you called "friend."

In the first century church, there were three controversial divisions that almost tore the infant congregations apart. They were:

- the controversy over male circumcision under the New Covenant;

- the controversy of Gentiles being accepted into the New Covenant;

- the controversy of animal sacrifices being offered at the Temple in Jerusalem.

At the church in Galatia, the people were in such disarray and disagreement over the importance of Jewish law versus their new freedom in Christ, that young Jewish and Gentiles Christians were "biting and devouring one another" (Gal. 5:15). We would say today, "They were chewing each other out." This caused division in the congregation, and Paul warned the Galatians to beware, lest they be consumed by one another.

MY PERSONAL STORIES

Many of you have lived with this experience, as I have. Many of you have found yourselves on both sides of this, as I have.

Decades ago, we dealt with a businessman who owed our ministry over twelve thousand dollars, but he chose to withhold it. This was a huge amount of money to us at that time. We could have hired an attorney and settled it in court. However, after much prayer, the Lord told me to treat it as a donation and let him keep the money. I obeyed the Lord, forgave the man, and held nothing against him. Soon after, we received an unexpected donation that more than compensated for what this man owed us.

I have also been on the side where individuals felt that I had wounded them, particularly because of decisions I made. They felt that I, or others involved, had somehow blocked God's will or ultimate destiny for them. In such instances, there is no sense in debating or arguing, as it only lights fires of contention. Instead, pray for these people to receive emotional, mental, and spiritual healing, which also helps release you from unforgiveness toward them.

The Bible is the "sword of the Spirit" (Heb. 4:12, Eph. 6:17). Carnally minded people take the sword and abuse people with it, using verses to attack others in the name of Christ. Knowing the warnings in scripture, I would never plot or set a trap of offense toward anyone. However, along with many of you, I have experienced wounds that I needed God to heal. Only when I released others who created the offense did my own wounds begin to heal.

People will never receive healing, so long as they are determined to hold onto offense and unforgiveness. We all have known people who seemed to enjoy soaking in a lake of offense, even quoting a Bible verse out of context to justify their position. The longer these people continue like this, the more bitter they become, the more they attack and criticize, the more attention they seek, the more they try to pull others into their offense, and the more they claim to do it all in the name of justice, righteousness, and the good of humanity.

However, when you examine their motives, you find that they are deep, dark, and impure. One man who claimed to be a minister did another minister as much harm as he could, later telling a friend that "God" told him to do it. If God told him to do it, it was not Almighty God; it was the "god of this world" (2 Cor. 4:4). When people tell you that God told them to do something, but their actions are contrary to God's instructions in His Word, you can be sure the instructions did not come from the Almighty.

HEALING YOUR WOUNDED SOUL

In Psalm 23, David wrote, "He (God) restoreth my soul." The Hebrew word for restore is *shub*, a word that means "to return, turn back, restore, repent." The word is also found in the Hebrew word Teshuvah, the time set aside each year when devout Jews prepare for the Day of Atonement and seek God for forgiveness, as well as forgive others.

The word restore refers to "making things as they were," including before the fall or the attack. Among the Greeks, the word *restitution* (Acts 3:21) is used. The picture is that of a doctor resetting a dislocated bone, thereby providing a healing process for a full recovery. Joel 2:25 notes that God will restore to you the years that the enemy has taken. This Hebrew word for restore is *shalam* (not shalom), which refers to making amends. We might say it means "to make up to you those years; to recompense (pay back) that which has been lost."

A restoration is not just to take you back to the place you were, but to restore the blessings that were lost because of the attack. When God brought restoration of Job's children, land, animals, and health, He blessed Job with twice as much as before (Job 42:10). The Bible even points out that his three daughters, born after his trial, were more beautiful than any throughout the land (Job 42:15).

SURROUNDED WITH THE RIGHT PEOPLE

During restoration, it is important to have the right spiritually minded people close to you. I am blessed to have an incredibly amazing wife, son, and daughter. I remember a time when my daughter would text me specific scriptures, almost daily, that the Lord placed on her heart to send to me while she was praying for me. It is astonishing to see how specific Bible verses can be so pertinent to your situation, as though they were written a few weeks ago. This shows us how the situations from thousands of years ago are so parallel to our own today.

One day when I was a bit despondent, I received a package in the mail. Inside was a stack of handwritten cards and letters. My daughter had gone to the youth at the Ramp in Hamilton, Alabama and said, "If my dad's ministry has ever blessed you in any way, write him a card or a note." There in each envelope were beautiful messages with amazing testimonies I had never heard. Sometimes we don't realize how one testimony, one card, or one letter can bring a powerful light of encouragement to someone who is discouraged.

Pam and I have some friends that we have known since they were children. Today they are adults who have their own children of all ages. Some have gone through traumatic events, including sickness, deaths, and marital crisis that sometimes felt unbearable. We have used our phones, a card with a note, or a small gift to remind them that Pam and I are standing with them, and so is the Lord. I recall how it felt to read a note about how my ministry had helped someone. A kind text, a note, a video, a card, or a letter has the potential to inject peace and joy into a wounded soul.

Healing and restoration of a wounded soul takes time. It always begins with forgiveness and releasing offense. It continues with prayer and study of the Word of God to renew your mind. If you know of someone who carries wounds from the past, instead of always bringing up the past, which only serves to rip off the bandage and remind them of the pain, be an encourager and a blessing. The blessings, love, and encouragement you sow will one day be returned to you in some manner.

CHAPTER 13

TURNING YOUR WEAKNESS INTO STRENGTH

There is a word in the New Testament that is often misunderstood. The word is *infirmity.* In the west, this word describes a serious medical condition, especially one that might cause difficulty with physical function. However, in the King James translation of the New Testament, the word infirmity is used seven times and the Greek word is *astheneia.* The word is translated as disease, infirmity, sickness, or weakness. Weakness alludes to an absence of strength. The weakness can be physical, mental, spiritual, or even moral.

In Luke 13, Christ encountered a woman who had been weak and bent over for eighteen years. Christ identified her as a daughter of Abraham (Luke 13:16), indicating that she was Jewish and had been faithful to worship and serve God. Christ immediately exposed the root of her years of suffering as a "spirit of infirmity" (Luke 13:11). This phrase can be interpreted as a "spirit of weakness."

Some physical frailties and weaknesses comes upon us as we age. It is a natural process that all people encounter to some degree. When I was about fifty-eight, my glucose was high and I was getting no exercise whatsoever. My wife asked a staff member to make me get up from my desk and walk the property. I remember the first afternoon when, once outside, the person took off jogging. I yelled, "Stop! I can't jog.

My legs won't cooperate. Just walk fast!" At age sixty-five, I told my wife that what does work has slowed down, and what once worked has retired. I have friends who say that the highlight of their day is taking a nap.

While we joke about age, dealing with an infirmity and a weakness can be a serious struggle. At times we know there is something happening in our mind or body, but we may not be aware of the source or the diagnosis.

WHY WAS I DIFFERENT?

In my teenage years, I had a strong love for God. I accepted God's call into the ministry at age sixteen and preached my first sermon at that age in Salem, Virginia where my dad pastored. At age eighteen, I received revival invitations in three states and began preaching nightly in these revivals. In some churches, the revivals continued for weeks.

In those days, the evangelist stayed in the home of either the pastor or a church member because rural areas had no hotels, and small churches had no extra income to house a guest speaker in a hotel, anyway. When I prepared to minister in a new location, a strong dread and anxiety would overwhelm me. I dreaded staying in someone's home. While I was there, I stayed in my room where I studied and prayed all day, or I went to the church where I could be alone and undisturbed.

I held a revival in 1977 at a church in Montcalm, West Virginia. The pastor told me years later that, during the three-week revival, I seldom came out of my room or even came to the table to eat. They were concerned about me. The fact was, I wanted to be left alone.

I felt stressed having to meet new people, and I was awkward in a conversation, unless the person was my age. Once I had known the person for a while, I would come out of my shell. Even throughout school, I made few friends. I was often called weird by other students and was severely bullied at times. There were nights when I had a hard time sleeping. Was I just shy, or was there something deeper going on?

Even to this day, at my VOE office (which is two large, connecting rooms), I am isolated away from the other offices. On average, I spend eight hours a day there during the week. I am happy to isolate in that one location, whether I'm writing, reading, or rummaging through sports cards. I seldom go into town for lunch. If someone interrupts my writing routine, I sense anxiety.

It's hard for me to be social, even when guests come to our house. I spend a little bit of time talking, then I go into my "man cave" to work on my laptop and watch a ballgame or *It's a Wonderful Life* for the two hundredth time. I have quirks that others notice that I tend not to see. I have a set routine that is almost impossible to break. Since my early years of ministry, I have had a routine of preaching in the same churches year after year, as routines are difficult for me to break. I will go back to the same church every year for fifteen to twenty years, and I stay fiercely loyal to my true friends who have been there for decades.

THE DIAGNOSIS

Decades passed and, after my son was diagnosed, tests revealed that I, too, am on the autism spectrum. Specifically, I was diagnosed with Asperger's syndrome, which is a high functioning autism. The condition is characterized by symptoms I experienced, such as repetitive patterns of behavior, intense preoccupation with a narrow interest, difficulty engaging in a typical back and forth conversation, difficulties with social interaction, and inflexibility with routines, yet without intellectual impairment or significant problems with verbal communication.

For anyone in full-time ministry, especially a pastor who must continually deal with people, these symptoms would be a serious challenge. For an evangelist who travels and deals primarily with staff, the situation is a bit different.

TAKING ADVANTAGE OF THE WEAKNESS

There are distinct disadvantages to being autistic, but there is also one distinct advantage with Aspergers. Since the person has the ability to focus so intensely on one interest and their intellect is not impaired, that allows the person who has discovered their primary interest to accomplish much more than could be done otherwise. This is how I have been able to do as much as I have in ministry. The counselor said that I have extreme focus and a questioning mind. I think more deeply about the questions, which has been a tremendous benefit while studying the Bible.

This helped me realize that these *weaknesses* I have are indeed a *strength,* once they are considered in the context of things they have allowed me to accomplish. Here are a few of the things I've done with the help of the Lord:

- spent seven years writing a million-word Bible commentary;

- have written around a hundred books and booklets since age eighteen, although I stopped counting;

- write articles for the quarterly VOE magazine, which has been printed for around forty-eight years;

- gather study material and tape YouTube videos each week;

- create messages and tape the Manna-Fest programs for fifty-two weeks of programming;

- oversaw the building of OCI, two VOE office buildings, and three additional buildings on the properties;

- spent over forty years traveling, preaching revivals, and conducting conferences where I sometimes preached six services over a weekend;

- write and record up to forty messages for every Israel tour.

Without a desire to isolate, without extreme focus, and without the ability to sustain a routine that would be boring to most people, much of that list would not have been possible. Instead of complaining about the weaknesses, I finally learned it was okay to embrace the abilities God imparted to me, and in doing so, have taken advantage of weakness.

STRENGTH IN WEAKNESS

Paul wrote in 1 Corinthians 2:3, *"And I was with you in weakness, and in fear, and in much trembling."* He said in Galatians 4:12-15, *Brethren, I urge you to become like me, for I became like you. You have not injured me at all. You know that because of physical infirmity I preached the gospel to you at the first. And my trial which was in my flesh you did not despise or reject, but you received me as an angel of God, even as Christ Jesus."* (NKJV)

Paul's infirmities, in part, were caused by a hindering spirit. Paul had been arrested, stoned, shipwrecked, beaten with rods, and physically abused. He wrote that he bore on his body the marks of being physically abused for the gospel (Gal. 6:17). The word "marks" is the Greek word *stigmata*, which alludes to being pierced or cut for recognition of ownership, and figuratively, it means "a scar for service." In

Paul's mind, he considered the scars he received from being beaten for the gospel to be a mark identifying him as a faithful and a true servant of Christ.

Paul also pointed out how he viewed his physical weakness that was caused by being punished for preaching the gospel:

> *"And he said unto me, My grace is sufficient for thee: for my strength is made perfect in weakness. Most gladly therefore will I rather glory in my infirmities, that the power of Christ may rest upon me. Therefore, I take pleasure in infirmities, in reproaches, in necessities, in persecutions, in distresses for Christ's sake: for when I am weak, then am I strong."*
>
> – 2 CORINTHIANS 12:9-10

How can you be strong when you are weak? From personal experience, we know that when we feel weak or helpless, we lean more on the Holy Spirit and place complete dependence upon the Lord as we walk in His presence.

This was Paul's secret. He and his ministry companion, Silas, were arrested, severely beaten, confined in wooden stocks, and locked in a dirty Roman prison. However, in their weakness, they began to sing worship songs to God, singing so loudly that the other prisoners could hear them. In their weakest and darkest moment, their praise began to rattle their cage, and an earthquake broke that which bound them. Their deliverance from prison did not erase their physical pain, but neither could their physical pain erase their desire to worship (Acts 16:22-31).

ACCEPT IT OR REJECT IT?

The question becomes, when should we accept a weakness or when should we reject it? The answer is found in asking the question: How does the weakness impact your life, and can it be altered? If that weakness is something such as drug addiction, alcoholism, pornography, or unclean habits, then all of these can be overcome through repentance, discipline, and walking in a redemptive salvation covenant. You can be cleansed and delivered by the power of the blood of Jesus Christ. We should never accept what God would reject, and neither should we reject what God would accept. Your body is the temple of the Holy Spirit (1 Cor. 3:16-17). God wants us to be free and cleansed from anything that defiles our bodies. Give the Holy Spirit unlimited access to dwell in righteousness, peace, and joy in a holy vessel (Rom. 14:17).

In a situation such as mine, I have prayed for God to help me in the areas where I am weakest. Yet, I understand that many of our ministry resources and accomplishments would not have happened without an ability to spend so much time alone and intensely focused on one thing. I no longer see my situation as a negative, because I am doing something I enjoy. It is not a drudgery to be doing something you enjoy, which is why I have been able to spend so much time studying the Bible and imparting what I have learned to others. Indeed, it is somewhat of an addiction, and I can relate to the experience of those in the house of Stephanas:

> "I beseech you, brethren, ye know the house of Stephanas, that it is the first fruits of Achaia, and that they have addicted themselves to the ministry of the saints."
>
> – 1 CORINTHIANS 16:15

Even in a case like this, it is important to maintain a balanced life. I have learned this the hard way after sitting at a desk for hours at a time, not exercising, not eating right, and suffering the health consequences.

THE SPIRIT HELPS US

Satan can and will take advantage of weaknesses of the flesh, which are often a side effect of lust of the flesh, lust of the eyes, and the pride of life (1 John 2:16). God has, however, provided a method for you to deal with such infirmities.

In Romans, Paul exposed the friction created by the flesh warring against the Spirit. Jesus noted that we should watch and pray that we enter not into temptation, as "the spirit is willing, but the flesh is weak" (Matt. 26:41). Jesus was in the Garden of Gethsemane when He made that statement to His three inner circle disciples, who were *sleeping* while He was experiencing mental agony.

In Romans, the Apostle Paul revealed a powerful revelation to help our weakness:

> *"Likewise the Spirit also helps in our weaknesses. For we do not know what we should pray for as we ought, but the Spirit Himself makes intercession for us with groanings which cannot be uttered. Now He who searches the hearts knows what the mind of the Spirit is, because He makes intercession for the saints according to the will of God."*
>
> – ROMANS 8:26-27 (NKJV)

The Holy Spirit helps our infirmities, or weaknesses. In this context, Paul was dealing with freedom from condemnation, as those whose sins are forgiven are new creations being led by the Holy Spirit. One weakness Christians have is not knowing *what* to pray. The Holy Spirit will help that weakness by standing in the gap to make intercession for us.

After years of exile and being hunted by his father-in-law, David noted, "I am weak this day, though anointed king" (2 Sam. 3:39). You can be anointed and still experience weakness. The Holy Spirit is assigned to be your helper in times of weakness. You can lean heavily on Him, as He will not collapse under the weight of your burden.

Part of the help provided is the gift of praying in the prayer language of the Spirit. The Holy Spirit knows the secret plans of the adversary and can expose them in advance. He also knows the perfect will of God and will help you achieve the goal of walking in God's purpose for your life.

When praying in the Spirit, your spirit is praying to God (1 Cor. 14:2,14). Paul taught that praying in the Spirit edifies (builds up) your inner spirit (1 Cor. 14:4). Jude wrote that believers build themselves up on their most holy faith when they pray in the Holy Spirit (Jude 20). These are just a few benefits of a Spirit-filled life.

When God brought you into this world, He factored in your strengths and weaknesses. He has given you a path to follow and the resources necessary to turn your weakness into strength.

CHAPTER 14

HAVE YOU EVER SAID, "THIS IS JUST WEIRD?"

In a previous chapter I mentioned the three types of spiritual tests or temptations—common, seasonal, and the hour of testing. A *common* test is one of many ordinary challenges that everyone deals with in life. A *seasonal* attack is one that reemerges after a period of time, including one that you thought you had gained victory over. The *hour of testing* (Rev. 3:10) is when "all hell breaks loose," leaving you stunned and unprepared for the most difficult challenge of your life.

Since the birth of the first century church, every generation has faced its own battles. The very first followers of Christ butted heads with idol worshippers when they preached that there was only one true God. Sometimes this stirred up entire cities against the messengers, leading to physical beatings and their arrest. In centuries that followed, Christians endured persecution unto death as history records ten Roman emperors who directed ten severe persecutions against believers. To live as a Christian in the second and third centuries was a risky choice that could lead to imprisonment or death.

Over time, wars occurred involving other religions. The Inquisition that began in the 12th century pitted Christians against other Christians, leading to violence and torture over doctrinal issues. Tests of the early church primarily involved religious persecution, but the generation living today is being challenged with *weird warfare*.

In the late 1980s and early 1990s, I was invited to preach at a church in California that had many members from Romania. Under communism, these believers had lived under daily pressure and dangerous persecution. Pastors often were arrested for preaching. The church operated underground for nearly forty years. Once communism fell, western secular media began to dominate the television networks, eventually influencing and altering the dress style, music, and attitude of the young people throughout much of Romania.

The Romanians living in California stated that it was easier to serve the Lord under communism and persecution in Romania than it was in the United States. They explained, "The only spirits we battled in Romania were poverty and persecution, and it kept us on our knees praying and seeking God. You could not survive without a daily prayer life of deep intercession. In America, there is no persecution and no level of suffering like we saw in Romania. The demonic spirits are different. Here there are seducing spirits and sexual perversion that create strong temptations. The opportunity to sin is always present. Temptations are much stronger in America than in a communist nation." Their warfare was once *persecution;* now it was *seducing spirits and sexual temptation.*

THE WEIRD WAR AMONG CHRISTIANS

In the book of Acts, a husband and wife named Ananias and Sapphira sold property and committed to bring a specific amount of the proceeds to the church to distribute among the needy. They presented a lesser offering and plotted to lie so they could keep more income for themselves. Their greed and lies cost them their lives (Acts 5:1-10). Why would two believers conspire to lie to an apostle about an offering?

When Saul was king of Israel, at times he would treat David as a son. Other times, Saul would throw javelins and attempt to slay this future king (1 Sam. 18:10-11; 19:10). This "split personality" was influenced by an evil spirit (1 Sam. 18:10). In the case of Ananias and Sapphira, Peter said that Satan had filled their hearts to lie (Acts 5:3). Some activities that believers engage in are difficult to explain unless an evil or unclean spirit is involved.

Years ago, two women in a local church began an intercessory ministry. Both had been converted to Christ and filled with the Holy Spirit, and both were considered strong in their faith. The two began to spend long amounts of time together, day after day and week after week. After several months, the two announced that they had become "lovers," to the shock and dismay of the congregation.

Thanks to a caring pastor and two husbands who refused to accept what they knew was a deceptive lie from a seducing spirit, spiritual authority was taken over the seducing spirit. The women ended their relationship, and their marriages were restored.

In a second example, a minister planned to hire a married couple to serve as minister of music at his church. When this young, attractive couple stepped off the plane, the pastor later confessed, "I felt something strange, just odd, coming from the young man, but I tried to put it out of my mind. I knew I should not have hired them, but there was a magnetic pull that continually played on my mind. I hired them despite the check I felt in my spirit."

Months later, the pastor and the young man became emotionally involved with one another, leading to an illicit relationship that was exposed and cost both men their ministries. By the grace of God, prayer, and counseling, the former pastor's wife remained with him. The soul tie with the young man was broken and eventually he was spiritually restored.

Throughout decades of full-time ministry and having preached in hundreds of churches of all sizes, I have heard some sad stories that involved sins within the church, which begs the question: How could someone with biblical knowledge open the door for such activity? How does a church experience everything from a bookkeeper stealing from the church's bank account to the youth pastor being arrested for child pornography?

While there is common temptation that involves certain emotions, mental tests, and challenges that all believers will encounter, some forms of iniquity far exceed the level of common temptation. The motivation must come from either negative carnal desires or an unclean spirit that attempts to bind the person into walking in disobedience. The problem could also be caused by troubles the person experienced early in life, issues and abuses the person never dealt with, which will also open the door to these evil spirits.

I knew of a married woman who, for several years, carpooled to and from work, an hour each way, with a married man (who later divorced his wife). The man "fell in love" with the married woman and was waiting for her husband to die so he could marry her.

Two married people carpooling to work might have seemed innocent at first, but frankly, it's a stupid idea. It is unlikely that a man and woman could be alone with each other five days a week, morning and evening for years, without getting too close. It is difficult enough for some people to work together in the same building. This sort of thing opens the door to temptations that can eventually end with divorce and divided families.

WHAT IS YOUR WEIRD WARFARE?

Weird warfare includes thoughts gripping your mind that you have never battled before. Over the years, strong and dedicated believers have contacted our ministry for prayer, as they shared that their mental thoughts were becoming a serious battle. This included voices telling them to kill themselves because life is not worth living. Some were locked in a cycle of believing they are not loved or that God has forsaken them, so they should just quit and give up. Others admit to temptations they never had dealt with before. One man who never drank alcohol began experiencing a strong desire to get drunk, just to see what it's like. I have met people who truly love God but must fight the mental assault that accuses them of having blasphemed the Holy Spirit.

Your battles might be different from someone else's, and perhaps you have never been tested with a fiery dart from the enemy (Eph. 6:16). If not, be assured that these mental assaults are real and quite distressing to those who have been hit with them.

THE SPIRIT OF DECEPTION

The primary end-time weapon that the kingdom of darkness never wants you to expose is their ability to *deceive*. Prophecy ministers turn to Matthew 24 when explaining the "signs of the times," but often overlooked is the most significant warning Christ gave His disciples. He warned four times in Matthew 24 to be on guard against deception (Matt. 24:4, 5, 11, 24). The Greek word for deceive is *planao*, meaning "to roam, to go astray (from safety and truth); to lead into error, to seduce."

Your greatest weapon against deception is truth, as accepting revelation of God's truth will set you free (John 8:32). In Hebrew the word for truth is *emet*, which is spelled with three Hebrew letters—alef, mem, and tav. The letter alef is the first letter of the Hebrew alphabet and is a letter that can represent God, who is the beginning of all things. If we remove the letter alef from the word *emet*, we get the word *met* which in Hebrew means *death*. This reveals a powerful truth. If we remove God and His truth, it will send us down a path of deception and eventual death.

The spirits assigned to deceive people are called seducing spirits (1 Tim. 4:1). The word for seducing is the Greek adjective *planos*, and it refers to a spirit that wanders around like a tramp and an imposter to lead people astray. Sometimes the King James Version of the Bible translates the word as deceiving.

The *root* of any deception is a lie, and to be deceived or seduced is to believe a lie. If the lie is maintained long enough in a person's mind, the lie can seem true to that individual. 0The Bible speaks of people who will not love the truth, and God will send them a strong delusion that they should believe the lie (2 Thess. 2:10-12).

Once someone embraces a lie long enough, the cement of deception will create a hardened heart. The assignment of a seducing spirit is to cause the conscience of an individual to become calloused against the convicting power of God's Word by strengthening lies that will eventually lead a person into spiritual, emotional, and mental captivity.

When addressing the church at Corinth, Paul said, "Let no man deceive himself" (1 Cor. 3:18). He used the word *exapatao*, which means, "to beguile thoroughly, to cheat, to deceive wholly." It describes someone who has been tricked and taken into captivity by Satan. *Exapatao* emphasizes the result once someone has fallen into the trap of deception. The process of deception begins by looking at the bait and moving toward it, but the consequence happens once the bait and hook have been swallowed.

First Timothy 4:1 warns that people will *give heed* to a seducing spirit and be deceived. Every spirit has a voice to plant words and seeds into the minds of those they attack. To give heed or take heed means to *pay attention to; give regard toward; be given over to.* These spirits fully attempt to seize your attention, plant a lie, and throw fiery darts in your mind. The enemy never shows the end result of the deception. If he did, his target might never fall for the lie.

EMOTIONAL ATTACHMENTS

The most powerful form of deception is one with strong emotions attached. For instance, some individuals who are involved in an alternative lifestyle may want to change; but a seducing spirit that has them attached to the other person works overtime to maintain the connection. Thus, it becomes more difficult for the one seeking freedom to sever the tie.

When this strong force between individuals is broken, some describe an almost death-like feeling that overwhelms them for a while. Paul might have been referring to this soul tie when he wrote: *"Or do you not know that he who is joined to a harlot is one body with her? 'For the two,' He says, 'shall become one flesh'"* (1 Cor. 6:16).

One way to help discern deception and protect yourself from it is to align your lifestyle and actions with the Word of God, not with your own desires or someone else's opinions. I grew up in a strict, full gospel church denomination that emphasized the importance of outward appearance. They were especially hard on women, as the church taught against wearing make-up, jewelry, and such. They also expected women to have long hair. A few New Testament scriptures were used out of historical context to defend the emphasis on outward appearance.

As time progressed, some of these strict ideas were noted as traditional preferences or customs, but not direct instructions for a person's lifestyle. But I remember that some parents were very strict on their children, demanding that they follow all the church's traditions. Once some of these children grew up and left home, they also left the church and never returned. One of my relatives said that, in her teens, the judgmental and critical attitudes in the church were so hateful that she finally said to herself, "If heaven is like these people, I don't want to go."

A couple people on one side of my family were so strict in the 1930s and 40s that—in the name of holiness—they so completely turned off some of their children to Christianity that the children left church as adults and never returned. The children were taught the *laws*, but they never discovered the *love* of God. Tradition was exalted above truth. Some people lived in constant fear that God was going to kill them if they didn't obey the traditions.

Clear, biblically-based spiritual regulations that our Heavenly Father places upon His children are not intended to strip us of our joy or to make life a boring journey. Consider the Ten Commandments, which some people think are a bondage, but are in fact given to us as a blessing. The commandments are summarized in this way: Love God with all your heart, soul, and mind, and love people as you love yourself (Matt 22:37-40).

When I was much younger, I assumed that the older a person is, the easier it would be to live for God and avoid certain trials or temptations. I learned that the trials did not end, but the ways in which they were plotted against us changed. There are some things that I have never been remotely tempted to do. The idea of smoking, drinking alcohol, or taking illegal drugs has never once interested me. I have always had high integrity when dealing with ministry finances, knowing that it all belongs to God and His kingdom. However, I have battled depression, feelings of rejection, and insecurity.

Tests and temptations are different for each person. But contrary to what we might have thought when we were young, advancing age doesn't abolish the battles. As long as we live, we will have the same flesh, and the adversary attacks people at every age. The enemy tempts so that we might sin or that our faith might fail. But God tests to reveal and sharpen our character. God doesn't test so that we will fail. We won't escape tests and temptations until our body is in a coffin and our spirit is in heaven.

Weird warfare is not an indication that you are "weird." It indicates that you're experiencing a different level of testing than what you are familiar with. Regardless of the level of testing and warfare, the weapons to defeat the weird always begin with the Word!

BE ACCOUNTABLE

In the book of Hebrews, we are given this instruction:

> *"Obey them that have the rule over you, and submit yourselves: for they watch for your souls, as they that must give account, that they may do it with joy, and not with grief: for that is unprofitable for you."*

> — Hebrews 13:17 (KJV)

It is important to be accountable to those who are over you in the Lord. Women tend to share their personal challenges with other women they trust. Men, however, think they are strong enough to fight their way through things on their own.

In the early 1990s, I was encountering severe mental depression, but told no one, thinking I would eventually pull myself out of it. When I could no longer handle it, I publicly revealed the problem when I suddenly stopped preaching during a tent revival. Immediately people came forward to pray for me, and a powerful spiritual intervention from God occurred through their prayers. Later my wife said, "I knew something was wrong, but why didn't you tell me what was happening?" I said, "I thought I could fight this on my own." Now, if weird warfare begins, we talk about it and pray with each other over the situation.

Many Christians, including ministers, have a problem trusting others when they are dealing with challenges. Several ministers have said, "I didn't feel like there was anyone trustworthy I could talk to."

This is an unfortunate problem in the church. People have extremely high expectations for *other* people, expectations they would never place on themselves. They also tend to be highly critical, especially of ministers. If they discover their demands and expectations have not been met, there's a self-righteousness about some people that makes them want to make sure everybody knows their opinion about the person's imperfections. They don't understand that people were humans before they were ever men and women of God. Moses became angry, Elijah experienced depression, and the list goes on.

Having someone to hold you accountable (or being an accountability partner) is not just about having a friend who will not gossip about you. It is about having one or more godly, trustworthy, loyal, praying friends who are full of wisdom, so that you can go to them in confidence and ask for prayer, advice, and guidance. It is also about you listening to them and being willing to correct areas of weakness.

Any problem that remains hidden in the dark is dealt with by bringing it into the light. When the light of God's Word shines in the darkness, the enemy has nowhere else to hide, and he can no longer conceal himself in darkness.

CHAPTER 15

HOW DOES THE ENEMY SET SNARES?

Ecclesiastes 9:12 (Amplified) reads, *"For man also knows not his time [of death]: as the fishes are taken in an evil net, and as the birds are caught in the snare, so are the sons of men snared in an evil time when [calamity] falls suddenly upon them."* A snare is a trap—think of a bird trap—of calamities and plots, with a source or agent behind it who set the trap.

I have never forgotten a certain six-month period of my early full-time ministry that began at age eighteen. I fasted often, prayed for long periods of time, and spent hours each day studying. This was the beginning of a ministry that has turned into nearly five decades of full-time traveling evangelism. As a teenager, it didn't take long for me to understand firsthand that all those scriptures and stories about demonic spirits were real and not just something that happened in Jesus' day.

THE DARK, HOODED SPIRITS

The strange activity began slowly and progressed into full blown encounters. The early attacks ranged from a bizarre itching sensation all over my body while I tried to sleep, to the bed being shaken, to audible voices waking me up. After a few months, I was being awakened by evil spirits dressed in black hooded robes with faces of utter darkness.

When I would tell other ministers what I experienced, they would look at me and grin. I could tell they thought the encounters were due to an overactive imagination. It made me realize that very few Christians ever experience these types of audible or visible occurrences, and for that they should be thankful.

Before a manifestation occurred, I would hear a buzzing noise in my ears and become physically paralyzed, followed by audible voices that would rage, curse, and threaten me. It was a life of mental torment, while at the same time, I was experiencing great revivals.

These manifestations continued off and on for six months, until December 31, 1978. I went to bed that night asking God to deliver me from this harassing demonic spirit. For the first time in weeks, I slept soundly. Then at three o'clock in the morning, I was abruptly awakened by a hand violently jerking my right leg, as if attempting to pull me out of bed. Then something strange happened. I saw a pleasant-looking male face appear a few feet from my face. His eyes looked full of compassion. I felt relieved, thinking that God must have sent an angel into my room.

But suddenly the face became contorted with an evil stare, followed by a hollow demonic laugh. This was no angel of God, but the visible face of a fierce evil spirit that was laughing at me in mockery. I know what the Bible means in 2 Corinthians 11:14 when it says that Satan transforms himself into an angel of light.

I felt a surge of righteous indignation. Instead of panicking and wanting to hide under the covers, my inner spirit rose up within me and I shouted out within my spirit (not with my voice, but with my mind), "No! That's enough! You will no longer torment me! I've had enough!" That was the Holy Spirit rising within me.

The evil spirit vanished and I was filled with peace and a fresh anointing. It felt like a weight had been lifted. Then the Holy Spirit gave me this word: *"Son, as long as you live, Satan will use what you see and what you hear against you. It is time that you stand on the only thing that can never be shaken or changed. Stand upon my Word."*

From that moment, the voices, appearances, and feelings of fear departed. I never saw another visible manifestation of a demonic spirit until November of 1981 when I watched one open a locked door and walk into the evangelist's quarters in a church.

My dad would refer to this as a "harassing spirit." Paul the Apostle would identify it as a "hindering spirit." In Paul's situation, the messenger of Satan (angel) was hindering him and continually buffeting him (2 Cor. 12:7). The word "buffet" refers to brutally beating and striking someone with a fist, and continuing the beating each time they get up. It is the same word used at Christ's trial, when soldiers beat Him with their fists and demanded that He prophesy (Mark 14:65).

WRONG THINKING

Wrong thinking in the western church has created an unbalanced perception of God and His Word. Some say that, if you are sick, then you must not have enough faith. Or, if you are financially struggling, you have not given enough in the offerings. I've heard that if your children are rebellious, you are a bad parent. If you fall into a snare, it was your own fault.

These are opinions that cannot be accepted as absolutes. This would be akin to Job's three friends telling Job that his horrible trial and losses happened because he was living in sin, or because he had too much pride and God plotted evil against him to bring him down a notch. God Himself rebuked Job's three friends and told them that they were all wrong.

The snares of the adversary operate in four ways:

- Snares are set behind your back, and you are suddenly caught unaware.

- Snares are set that you see, but you are not sure how to get around it.

- Snares are set that you can see, but you continue in that direction anyway.

- Snares are sometimes permitted by God to see how you will respond.

At times snares come without any spiritual or logical explanations. However, the enemy sets a snare for one reason—to defeat you or destroy your confidence and faith in God.

THE IMPACT OF A SNARE

Once a Christian has been caught in a satanic snare, the result can be an emotional, moral, or spiritual crisis. If you are not a minister or church leader, then why is your failure so important? Here's why. The crisis affects more people than just you. It impacts others who are close to you. When one soldier in war is seriously injured, it can take at least two other soldiers away from the battle to assist the one wounded. A serious wound can impact at least three soldiers.

King David's family was close. But the time came when his sons began to work against him and they distanced themselves from their father. Whether out of anger or disappointment, the normal father-son relationships were severed.

Over a period of about twenty-two years beginning in 1980, at least ten different church leaders experienced some kind of minor or major ministry scandal. Two of the mega churches that had been featured on the cover of a Christian magazine eventually disbanded due to internal or financial crisis. The disappointment in the hearts of Christians can never be underestimated

When this happens, whether it was self-inflicted or designed by dark satanic angels, it creates these negative responses:

- Believers become *distracted* by the fog of war.

- Believers become *discouraged*, with some even thinking that if a leader falls, they themselves have no chance of making it.

- Believers fall into *disarray*, which often leads to a church split or internal divisions.

- Believers become *doubtful* of the anointing.

- Believers turn to *disinformation* to gain whatever news they can find about the situation.

- Believers allow their own testimony to be *disrupted* because of embarrassment.

THE AGE OLD ENIGMA

The puzzling question for people becomes: How can good men and women do such things? How can a praying Christian still be deceived? The scriptures explain:

> *"Now the Spirit speaketh expressly, that in the latter times some shall depart from the faith, giving heed to seducing spirits, and*

doctrines of devils; Speaking lies in hypocrisy; having their conscience seared with a hot iron."

— 1 Timothy 4:1-2 (KJV)

One of the strong dark angels in the enemy's kingdom is identified as a "seducing spirit." The modern definition implies sexual seduction, but the biblical word in Greek has a different meaning. The Greek word *planos* means "a tramp, an imposter, a misleader, a deceiver." In the context of that verse, Paul was warning Timothy of Christians being deceived and turning away from true, sound doctrine. They were being seduced into following doctrines of devils. They were even forbidding to marry, which is a covenant that God ordained (Heb. 13:4).

A seducing spirit also will mislead a person into believing that their actions are acceptable or even justified, despite the Bible teaching the contrary. Someone under the spell of a seducing spirit will manifest pride and anger, and even make threats when they are confronted with the truth. They will engage in unbiblical and unreasonable behaviors to manipulate and pressure you; for example, they might not allow you to see your grandchildren until you change your beliefs. Even the judicial system in some states will withhold children from one or both parents if the parent refuses to go along with something that will be harmful to their child—such as gender therapy.

THE TWO TYPES OF SNARES

One word for snare (*pagis*) means "to trap," such as one who sets a trap for catching birds. This kind of trap is visible but is walked into anyway. Like the bird, the person wants what's inside the trap. Another word that is translated snare (*brochos*) is a restriction or a restraint, such as a noose or a slip knot. One snare is walked into with your eyes open, while the other is hidden. Jesus said to *watch* and pray, lest you enter into temptation (Mark 14:38) It is one thing to see a trap in front of you and keep walking into it, but it is another thing to suddenly find a noose dropped around your neck.

King David sinned with Bathsheba and walked into a *pagis* trap. Samson's eyes latched onto a Philistine woman named Delilah who was used to lure from Sampson the secret to his strength. He walked into a *pagis* trap. A *pagis trap* is designed to appeal to your emotions and senses and to feed the flesh.

The *brochos* trap is concealed from view and well hidden—until you are captured in the ropes. The book of Job describes this snare:

> *"For he is cast into a net by his own feet, and he walks into a snare. The net takes him by the heel, and a snare lays hold of him. The noose is hidden for him on the ground, and a trap for him in the road."*
>
> – Job 18:8-10 (NKJV)

These traps are often set by people:

> *"The proud have hid a snare for me, and cords; they have spread a net by the wayside; they have set gins [traps] for me. Selah."*
>
> – Psalm 140:5 (KJV)

Snares can be set years in advance. This might be why we see certain patterns in families, such as the twelve-year sequence on my maternal side of the family. Is it possible that a plan can be laid out that far in advance, yet not acted upon for twelve years? Yes, because for the plot to succeed, certain circumstances must be lined up in advance.

In 2024, during the war with Hezbollah, the Israelis exploded around five thousand pagers and walkie talkies that were being carried by men affiliated with the terrorist organization. The Israeli plan was so elaborate that it took ten years from the time of planning to the time of activation. The strategy required detailed planning, secrecy, extreme patience and awareness, and expert military intelligence to make sure the enemy purchased the devices and remained unaware of what was coming.

SNARES YOU MAY ENCOUNTER

The most common snare is the *cares of life*. Second Timothy 2:4 tells us that "No one engaged in warfare entangles himself with the affairs of this life...." The word entangle describes a person who gets their feet tangled in vines while they're walking and trips or falls as a result.

Christ noted that the cares of life choke the Word (Mark 4:19). The Greek word for cares simply means *distractions* as well as things that *divide*. At times we take on more cares, when instead, we should be releasing cares. I think about friends who worked hard all their lives, invested for a great retirement, made plans to travel the world, and yet they passed away unexpectedly. They were never able to enjoy the fruit of their labors.

THE SNARE OF WEARINESS

Excessive cares of life include overwork and daily stress that locks a person into a trap of weariness. For too many years, I spent many hours each day in front of a laptop, doing work that required me to use my brain. This verse in Ecclesiastes 12:12 explains the result: *"Much study is a weariness of the flesh."*

At age eighteen, the Holy Spirit dropped Galatians 6:9-10 in my spirit when I became weary traveling non-stop: *"And let us not be weary in well doing: for in due season we shall reap, if we faint not."* The word weary in this verse simply means "weak or faint in heart." The word faint means weariness to the point of laying aside the desire to continue the fight.

In the Bible, Samuel anointed David as a teenager. He accepted a future assignment to be Israel's king. In the latter years of his life, David was weary and wrote, "I am weak this day, though anointed king" (2 Samuel 3:39).

No doubt some readers, at least those who have reached an upper age, can relate to that. I certainly can.

I accepted the call of God into the ministry at age sixteen. By age eighteen, I knew my assignment would be that of a traveling revivalist and evangelist. At the time, I wrote out a vision to form a 7-Point Outreach that would eventually impact the world. Decades passed, and growth of the ministry required more staff, land, buildings, income, and walking through more open doors. Unfortunately, I did not know how to slow down or what it meant to rest. I wore out my body to the point of burnout.

We must "labor to enter into rest" (Heb. 4:11). The word labor means "to make an effort, to strive, to be diligent." I must make myself rest, or else I would work nonstop. For a workaholic or a person who enjoys activity or staying busy, it takes effort to stop and say, "Today I'm taking a break from everything." Many pastors of large churches have learned to take time off throughout the year because they need to restore their vision and recharge their spirits.

THE SEX TRAP

Believers often assume that those outside the church have problems maintaining sexual purity, and there is much evidence in today's culture that this is true. It was true in biblical times as well. In Proverbs chapter 7, Solomon describes the woman who set out to seduce a young man:

"So she caught him, and kissed him, and with an impudent face

said unto him, I have peace offerings with me; this day have I payed my vows. Therefore, came I forth to meet thee, diligently to seek thy face, and I have found thee.

"I have decked my bed with coverings of tapestry, with carved works, with fine linen of Egypt. I have perfumed my bed with myrrh, aloes, and cinnamon. Come, let us take our fill of love until the morning: let us solace ourselves with loves. For the goodman is not at home, he is gone a long journey: He hath taken a bag of money with him, and will come home at the day appointed.

"With her much fair speech she caused him to yield, with the flattering of her lips she forced him. He goeth after her straightway, as an ox goeth to the slaughter, or as a fool to the correction of the stocks."

– PROVERBS 7:13-22 (KJV)

This woman intended to seduce the unnamed fellow while her husband was on a business trip. She noted that she had gone to God's house and given a peace offering. She also had paid her vows. It appears that this was a Jewish woman who was active at the temple and made sure she followed the Torah laws. In her mind, she was paying in advance for what she was about to do. It would be akin to you praying, "Lord, I am going to sin, so forgive me in advance before I do."

Forgiveness does not work that way, and her attitude would be called "presumptuous sin." David asked God to "keep back your servant also from presumptuous sins" (Psa.19:13). A presumptuous sin is one in which a person intentionally acts against what they know is right. In this woman's case the sinning woman felt her offerings at the temple had covered the sin she planned to commit before she committed it.

After David sinned, note what David *did not* do. He did not excuse his actions by saying, "None of this ever would have happened if she had not been bathing on her roof where I could see her." He did not say, "She didn't have to come to the palace. That was her choice." He did not say, "She seduced me. She forced me into the situation." David's wife, Michal, was Saul's daughter and she was not favorable toward David. The easiest excuse would have been, "It's my wife's fault. She never gives me attention, she mocks my worship, and she's just like her stubborn father."

David said none of those things. His response was, "Against You, You only, have I sinned" (Psa. 51:4). David repented: *"And David said unto Nathan, I have sinned against the LORD. And Nathan said unto David, The LORD also hath put away thy sin; thou shalt not die"* (2 Sam. 12:13 KJV).

After he repented, David sought God's restoration. He said, *"Restore unto me the joy of thy salvation. And uphold me with thy free spirit. Deliver me from blood guiltiness…"* (Psa. 51:12, 14). David recovered, indicated by the fact that the last Psalms are songs of praise.

LESSONS TO LEARN

God is never taken by surprise. Just as in Job's case, He is fully aware of every strategic plan of adversity coming toward you before it arrives. The second lesson is that there are times, especially during an intense or destructive conflict, that the adversary enacts his limited strategy with the permission of God, such as in Job's situation. Third, God has already planned your breakthrough in advance, and He is not struggling to figure out how to help you.

During these times it becomes necessary to lean fully on the Lord. *"Trust in the Lord with all you heart, and lean not on your own understanding. In all your ways acknowledge Him, and He shall direct your paths"* (Prov. 3:5-6).

CHAPTER 16

COUNTERATTACK—THE MANIFESTATION OF RETALIATION

S trong Christians will survive an initial conflict. However, sometimes they are unprepared for the counterattacks. When you have regained ground after an attack, the enemy sometimes unexpectedly returns with another attack to once again try to steal what doesn't belong to him. The counterattack explains why, after you gain victory, the battle seems to recycle again.

Throughout life I have observed two times in which adversity became stronger: *After a great victory, or before a great breakthrough.*

When David settled in Jerusalem, the Philistines immediately tested his resolve by gathering their forces on the west side of the city, in the Valley of Rephaim (literally, the valley of the giants). David amassed his troops and defeated the invaders. Then came the counterattack. The Philistines regrouped and moved their forces back in. It was the same valley and different soldiers, but the same source—the Philistines.

David was instructed to use a different strategy during the counterattack. God's war chariots went before David above the tops of the mulberry trees, supernaturally engaging the armies of the enemy. After this second attempt, the Philistines realized they could never defeat David, so they stopped trying (see 2 Samuel 5). The enemy had attempted to return after David's great victory to steal the victory from him. But the Lord went before him and struck the army of the Philistines.

Daniel 7:25 records one of the end-time goals of the kingdom of darkness: He shall wear out the saints of the Most High. This portion of Daniel was written in Aramaic. The phrase "wear out" is *bela* and is used only in the sense of oppressing and mentally wearing a person down. David described it as being at "wits' end" (Psa. 107:27). This phrase means to be at the end of wisdom, or in other words, you have tried everything you know to do and there is nothing left to do. You are too weary to fight, and you accept that it is what it is.

David spent many years trying to protect himself from a jealous King Saul. He had to flee and live as an outlaw until Saul finally died. Hopefully you never have to deal with someone who, like King Saul, has been overtaken by a tormenting spirit. These people become obsessed with retaliation and will do everything in their natural ability to wreak havoc. Even if they appear to stop long enough to take a vacation, they'll be back. I have observed people who seem to get a thrill from creating confusion and chaos, with some even claiming they have been selected as a special agent of God to do things that God either would not or could not do.

The ultimate sign of deception is when someone enacts a wicked and malicious plan, claiming they are doing it in God's name. Jesus warned that the time will come when a person will kill someone and think they are doing service unto God (John 16:2). Once people have been this strongly deceived by a false spirit, it is almost impossible for them to believe they are wrong. That is deception on steroids.

I once dealt with the most self-righteous man I had ever known. He bragged that he never attended church because he couldn't find one good enough. He would not attend any ministry related events, yet he described himself as a follower of Christ. At the same time, he followed a deranged woman on the internet who had been investigated as a fraud and felon, and he boasted about her as though she were the divine voice of God, even referring to her as a prophetess.

Despite hundreds of court documents implicating this woman, she has a faithful and radicalized following, some of whom claim to be Christians. This reminds me of Christ's warning that, in the end, if it were possible, even the very elect will be deceived (Matt. 24:24).

WHEN A DISEASE RETURNS

In ninth grade I played football in junior high school. In the middle of the season, I became sick. It felt as though there were pins in my brain, and it hurt when I moved.   My mother worked for a family doctor, and he was concerned that I could have meningitis. I took some pain medicine and missed three days of practice. But I decided to dress out and play the football game without telling the coach I was sick. After the game, I went home and collapsed. I found myself in a more serious situation than before. However, during a revival service, I was prayed for and was instantly healed.

One year later, the same month and same week in October, I was again hit with similar symptoms, and it took some time for me to recover. The year after that, twelve months later, I was struck yet again with the same infirmity.

By that time, I had been studying the Bible. And instead of taking medicine, I used the "gos pill" (the Gospel) and began to firmly and with strong faith rebuke this attack. I still remember taking a shower and stepping out completely healed.

This taught me that adversity can strike at the same time each year. I also learned the power of praying and speaking God's Word.

We could have a serious disease and experience God's supernatural healing, or we could receive a cure through medical treatment. Sometimes people have such a fear of the affliction returning that they will not even speak or testify that they are healed! Yet, scripture indicates that we overcome by the blood of the Lamb and the word of our testimony (Rev. 12:11).

One minister told a friend of mine who received a clean bill of health after a bout with cancer, "Now, be careful saying you're healed because it might come back." That's like advising, "Don't tell anyone you're a born again Christian because you might fall into sin again one day."

That advice contradicts the biblical statement regarding testimony. In the New Testament Greek, the word testimony is "judicial evidence given by a witness in a court." You testify because you have witnessed an event. The event was that Christ redeemed you or that Christ healed you. The firsthand testimony of a witness stands in a court case. The witness is providing evidence because they were there to see it, hear it, or experience it. The witness is not repeating what someone else said. The witness is telling what the witness personally experienced.

Just as fear can open a door to the problem returning, faith can keep the door closed and locked. Faith casts the mountain into the sea (Matt. 17:20).

WHAT IF SOMETHING RETURNS?

If a Christian has testified to being saved, yet they sin again, there is an answer for that. 1 John 2:1 says, *"My little children, these things I write to you, so that you may not sin. And if anyone sins, we have an Advocate with the Father, Jesus Christ the righteous."*

Jesus is our Advocate (our "heavenly lawyer") if we sin. But we don't run around saying, "I might fall, I might fall, I might sin." Instead, we confess, "I'm saved, my name is in the book of life, I love Jesus, and

I'm going to serve Him." Repentance, confession, and obedience to the Word are the keys to our salvation (Rom 10:10).

When David fought Goliath, he carried in his pouch five smooth stones. The Bible names five giants who were in Israel at that time. David was prepared to slay Goliath, along with the four other giants if necessary (1 Sam 17:40; 1 Chron. 20:4-8). Goliath had a brother named Lahmi (1 Chron. 20:5). Though Goliath was dead, Lahmi was alive and had to be slain later.

The spiritual pattern here is that God will help you slay a giant in your life. The giant is defeated and will not return. Yet, years later something shows up that looks and acts like the giant you defeated in the past. It is not Goliath back from the dead; it is a brother who looks a lot like Goliath. But there are still stones in the brook. The same faith you used to defeat past problems is the same faith you use to take on future challenges.

Every major attack that you overcome is often followed with counterattacks. David fought the first battle against the Philistines in Jerusalem in a traditional manner. During the counterattack, God changed the strategy by using angels. David experienced the same outcome—victory over his enemies.

THE ABILITY TO REMAIN UNMOVABLE

In Ephesians chapter 6, Paul provided the believer with a description of spiritual armor for use in any conflict. He instructed us, "Having done all to stand (in battle), keep standing" (Eph.6:13-14). In Paul's time, the leather shoes of Roman soldiers had metal spikes on the soles. This enabled them to stand on a hill, dig in, and fight, thereby giving them the advantage of being able to stand upright. When adversity persists, with hindrances, crisis, trauma, and cares of life, dig in and make up your mind to stand in faith, nothing wavering. A soldier who quits will go down in defeat.

Satan can be persistent, and those whom he motivates against you will be persistent, too. Just when you think the trial has ended, the adversary will agitate one of his minions to relight the fading embers. Satan's human minions are often people whom psychologists would describe as having certain emotional and behavioral disorders. Their actions draw attention to themselves, and they thrive on being noticed, even for the wrong reasons. They also experience a thrill from thinking they've made their target suffer. A clue that it's demonically inspired is that your attacker becomes angry when they see they're having little to no success in using their fiery darts to burn up your shield of faith.

I had the misfortune of being targeted by such a woman who lives halfway across the country and uses her social media platforms as a megaphone to spread libel and slander in the form of outrageous, defamatory lies. She targets well-known ministers, churches, musicians, and other Christian leaders because she's discovered that using their names causes naïve Christians to follow her, spread her lies, and thereby draw even more attention to her platforms.

The woman boasts by saying, "See, I'm telling the truth! Nobody's suing me!" The truth is that she *has* been sued for defamation by two people, one being her ex-husband. It's no small feat for a man to win a defamation lawsuit against his own ex-wife. The woman who brags that she's never been sued has not only *been sued*, she also committed bankruptcy fraud and fled the state to avoid paying the defamation judgments.

Most targets of her vicious assaults have important things to accomplish for God and His Kingdom. They don't waste time and money responding to satanically inspired nonsense and hauling demonically inspired people into court. The consensus among most Christian leaders is that this woman, who has an extensive history of criminal behavior that spans several states, has long ago been turned over to a reprobate mind (Rom. 1:28). She has sealed her own eternal destiny. Her punishment is not a lawsuit. Her punishment, if she never repents and turns from her wickedness, is eternal damnation, as *"All liars will have their part in the lake that burns with fire and brimstone"* (Rev. 21:8). That is much worse than any punishment meted out by an earthly judicial court.

Even though I had never heard of this woman until people called our office to report her initial attacks, I became a target of her vile absurdities and accusations. This continued for two or three years, and I'm told it continues to this day. She learned that our ministry has a protective storm shelter that houses our computer servers in the event of a tornado or other damaging weather. We spent a lot of money to purchase our own servers, and our information technology staff decided we should protect them as much as possible.

This woman concocted a whopper of a tall tale, assuring her followers that she has ironclad proof that we have victims chained up as slaves underground, and that the reason we aren't in prison is because we've paid off every law enforcement agent in America, from local police to the FBI in Washington. She cannot submit proof of any of her claims, since it's all a delusion that was fabricated by a deranged mind. Regardless, there are simple-minded people who believe everything she says, no matter how outrageous.

Inexplicably, she has alleged *Christian* followers who also believe everything she says. One of them trespassed on our ministry property and was recorded yelling, "Hello! Hello!" into a pipe that extended from the ground. Apparently, she expected to hear "Help! Help!" from people that she had been convinced were chained inside. To her credit, the trespasser apologized.

The woman who concocts the tales about ministers and ministries was professionally investigated, which included the acquisition of Freedom of Information police and court documents. Through the investigation she was exposed for a plethora of crimes, some federal, and for raising money fraudulently. Gullible people had forked over hundreds of thousands of dollars to her various personal online accounts using platforms such as GoFundMe and GiveSendGo.

One would think that any normal person with an average or above IQ would recognize that her stories are tall tales being crafted for a following and for profit. But there indeed are people claiming to be Christians who follow her and even affirm her posts. My wife and I know people who claim to be Christians who follow her, affirm her comments, and repost her tall tales. Sometimes you are compelled to ask yourself how certain individuals weaseled their way into your orbit.

That is one extreme example of deception that has overdosed on steroids, with people who call themselves Christians intentionally running straight into an obvious trap. The blind are leading the blind.

THE FISH DREAM

Pam and I have understood the importance of standing in silence and allowing God to fight battles. A few years ago, I was preaching in Kentucky when God gave me a spiritual dream. The quick summary of the dream is that I was in a boat with Evangelist Nik Walker, and we were attempting to catch fish in a lake. We observed that something was frightening the fish away from the net. I went under the water and saw six large fish lined up next to each other. They were operating "under the current" by using their mouths to prevent us from catching the fish. I hit one of the fish with a landing net, and eventually one fish rolled over and was dragged away by another fish. This caused the other fish to back up. As they backed up, I saw another fish in the distance that was hanging upside down on a hook.

The Holy Spirit told me the people whom each fish represented. He showed me that one of the fish was behind a plot that would be overturned. I believe the fish on the hook was the demonically inspired woman, and she would be "hung" by her own lies. A few years later, the dream was fulfilled. We dealt with constant battles, but Pam and I learned that the primary thing is to keep our hearts aligned with God's Word and keep ourselves free from offense and unforgiveness.

Spiritual and human adversaries will strike, then back up, then strike again, then step back until they attack again. They're hoping and waiting for you to fall, fail, or faint. Do not think it strange when an answer to prayer comes, a victory is gained, and you are hit again, perhaps even a third time. Christ was tempted three times back-to-back. What should you do when this happens?

First, rejoice and be thankful for every victory, healing, or prayer answered, and never allow anyone or anything to steal the joy of that moment. If a counterattack comes, remember the first victory and remind yourself that God won the first time, and He will initiate a second and third conquest on your behalf.

A third point is found in 1 Samuel 7:13 (KJV), *"So the Philistines were subdued, and they came no more into the coast of Israel: and the hand of the LORD was against the Philistines all the days of Samuel."* Instead of the enemy wearing down Israel, Israel wore out the enemy, and the hand of the Lord was against the Philistines. Any trial, test, or temptation cannot last forever. They all have an expiration date. It might last forty days, six months, or even years, because the hour of testing could be extended. Recall that *"Weeping may endure for a night, but joy comes in the morning"* (Psa. 30:5).

CHAPTER 17

SATAN'S MOST EFFECTIVE
UNDETECTED WEAPON

Years ago, a minister found himself entangled in self-invited legal trouble. At that time, a noted secular author had written a best-selling self-help book that was being read by tens of thousands of people. During a large Christian conference, an attendee informed this minister, who was a conference speaker, that the self-help speaker had recently committed suicide. When the minister spoke at the conference, he innocently mentioned the book and the suicide of the author.

Before long, the minister was contacted by the author's lawyers, advising him that the author was very much alive. They informed the minster that the statement he made fell into the legal application of public defamation. The minister found himself embroiled in a multi-million-dollar lawsuit with the author of the book and his publisher.

I personally met this minister who explained to me the lengthy legal battle that followed. It became the worst nightmare of his life. He repeated what he had been told, and instead of vetting the accuracy of the story, he repeated a lie. The legal battle continued for some time.

Sometimes publicly sharing information you heard from other people can get you in serious legal trouble. Christians are prone to doing this, sometimes under the guise of making their "concerns" known to others when, in fact, some of them simply enjoy spreading gossip. Unless you hear information directly from the mouth of the person you are talking about, you might be repeating a lie that could lead to legal ramifications.

The worse this kind of thing becomes with the popularity of social media platforms, the more lawsuits you will see against purveyors of slander and libel. With available technology today, people need to understand that a legal team could be monitoring everything you post or say anywhere online. Nothing posted on the internet ever disappears, even when it is deleted. Artificial intelligence technology can also be used against you in ways you never expected.

I NEVER SAID THAT

In the mid-1980s, I was preaching at a great church in my town. New information had come out of Israel concerning an archeological excavation in Qumran where they hoped to find an ancient jar of the "ashes of the red heifer." According to the Torah in Numbers 19, these ashes were required for ritual purification. Rabbis teach that the ashes of a red heifer will be needed in the future when a Jewish temple is rebuilt in Jerusalem. I thought this was intriguing, so I researched the subject and preached an unusual and detailed message to the congregation. That night the pastor was not there, as he had a family emergency.

Not long after that I received a call that there was some confusion over my message, and the pastor was upset. It was rumored I had stated that Jesus cannot return for the church until the ashes of the red heifer are discovered. This rumor spread near and far, and I was being called a heretic by a few denominational ministers.

I knew I had not said this, because I don't even believe that. I would never preach something I don't believe. I carefully listened to a copy of the message on cassette and, as I thought, that statement was never made or implied. Yet, it was repeated over and over as ministers said, "Perry is going off into heretical Jewish teaching."

An untruth was repeated without anybody investigating the facts, and investigating the facts would have been as simple as listening to a cassette tape recorded at the church. This message remained the most controversial of my ministry, until Time magazine published an article on the possible rebuilding of a Jewish Temple and the need for the ashes of the red heifer. A few people called me after that and apologized. This taught me that some people criticize any teaching they don't understand or have never heard before.

When I was younger, I would not confront anyone for making a false statement about me, as I felt it was persecution for the sake of the gospel. I was told that being misunderstood comes with the territory, or that this is all part of God's work. However, as I grew older and observed or experienced the damage done by backbiters, bold busybodies, and goofy gossipers, I reversed my position. I have learned that it is okay to confront a person when they are gossiping, which often surprises them because they aren't expecting you to challenge them.

I have low tolerance for anyone who willfully spreads lies. It's puzzling how someone who considers themselves a Christian, and especially someone involved in ministry, will pride themselves on their own righteousness, even bragging that their past is covered by the blood, yet they will tongue lash others with no consideration of Christ's warning to *"Judge not, and you will not be judged; condemn not, and you will not be condemned"* (Luke 6:37) and *"For with what judgment you judge, you will be judged; and with the measure you use, it will be measured back to you"* (Matt. 7:2).

IT'S NOT WHAT IT SEEMED

The words that slip from your mouth and begin with, "Have you heard?" nearly always open a door to suspicion, gossip, backbiting, and negativity. Most churches in America have a loosely knit "saints' rumor mill" where people gossip endlessly under the guise of fellowshipping. Untold eternal damage has been done by unvetted and untrue rumors. The following stories illustrate the dangers.

When the internet first became popular, our ministry was advised to set up our ministry website using the ".org" option and not ".com" because at that time, "com" was for corporations and "org" was for organizations such as churches and non-profits. We set up our website as voe.org and made the mistake of not reserving voe.com.

Time passed and we suddenly received phone calls from people telling us that they would no longer support us because of the porn on our website. Other people said they accidentally typed in our website as .com and were taken to a porn site that also included some of our ministry material! The site placed malware on their computer that had to be professionally removed.

After an investigation, we learned that someone overseas had purchased our name under the ".com" site and even used pictures of some of our ministry products along with their porn. We were not able to legally challenge the web owner because he was operating overseas. We had to depend on Aunt Bea and our Daughters of Rachel to pray this fraudster out of business.

It was shocking to think that people would believe we had porn on our webpage. But the fact that the fraudster was able to use our name enabled him to fool some people.

RUMORS BASED ON PROPHECY

The etymology of the word *rumor* is interesting. In Latin, the word means, "noise, clamor, common talk, or heresy." In French, the word means, "commotion, widespread noise, or something reported." The word is related to *ravus,* the word for "becoming hoarse in the voice because of bellowing out." We could say that a rumor is noise or clamor bellowed out that can cause commotion and may or may not be true.

The Bible gives an example of a religious rumor. When the angel Gabriel predicted John the Baptist's birth, he told John's father that John will "go before Him in the spirit and power of Elijah, to turn the hearts of the fathers to the children" (Luke 1:17). About four hundred years earlier, the prophet Malachi predicted that Elijah would return in the future and "turn the hearts of the fathers to the children and the hearts of the children to the fathers" (Mal. 4:5-6).

When John began his public ministry at age thirty, there was confusion in religious circles about whether he was the literal Elijah. There are sixteen recorded miracles in Elijah's ministry. John never performed a single miracle; he only baptized believers.

Christ's own disciples questioned Him about this Elijah connection to John. Christ had said, "Elijah is coming first and will restore all things" (Matt. 17:11). Christ also noted, "Elijah has already come, and they did not know him but did to him whatever they wished" (Matt. 17:12). The point is that there was division among religious people about John's identity. John was not *the* Elijah, but he did come with the same authority of the Old Testament prophet, Elijah.

Jesus asked His disciples "Who do men say that I, the Son of Man, am?" They answered, "Some say John the Baptist, some Elijah, and others Jeremiah or one of the prophets" *(Matthew 16:14 NKJV).*

This was a strange answer. His name was Jesus (Yeshua in Hebrew) and He was called Christ, which means "the anointed one." In Christ's day, the religiously inclined had set their prophetic interpretation of events and created a confusing mixture. John the Baptist had been beheaded, yet Herod believed that Jesus was John who had come back from the dead (Matt. 14:2). Others said Christ was Elijah, yet Elijah was a grown man when he was transported alive into heaven in a whirlwind and a chariot of fire. Jesus had been born as an infant in Bethlehem and did not descend from heaven as a full-grown man. A few believed Christ was Jeremiah, an Old Testament prophet who had died hundreds of years before Christ's appearance. No wonder the religious folks misunderstood Christ's teachings; *they didn't even know who He was!*

WHEN A RUMOR LEADS TO DEATH

Rumors can be dangerous enough to cost someone their life. In Paul's day, Nero was the Roman Emperor. This wicked and perverse dictator ordered the first deadly persecutions against Christians. In Rome, Nero allegedly hatched a plan to remove the various gods in Rome's temples and replace them with carved images of himself. He planned to rename Rome "Neropolis," meaning "City of Nero." The Roman Senate rejected the idea.

Tradition indicates that in anger, Nero sent men to set fire to the Roman markets (Circus Maximus). The fires burned for six days, destroying about seventy-five percent of the shops. Out of fear of retaliation from the Senate and Roman citizens, Nero needed a scapegoat, so he blamed the fires on Paul and the Christians living in Rome.

Before the fires, Paul had made a dangerous sea journey to Rome, then spent two years in a house with his own hired servants where no man hindered him (Acts 28:31). By accusing Paul, Nero found the perfect scapegoat, as Christians believed in another Kingdom—the Kingdom of God—and another King, Jesus Christ. Rumors circulated throughout the empire that one day the Christians would overthrow the Roman government and create a new kingdom.

What is so disheartening is that Nero's big lie spread throughout the Roman Empire, including Asia, where Paul had spent many years preaching and organizing new churches. Many Christians throughout Asia believed the lie that Paul was responsible for the fire. Notice the influence that Paul's ministry made upon Asia:

> *"Moreover you see and hear that not only at Ephesus, but throughout almost all Asia, this Paul has persuaded and turned away many people, saying that they are not gods which are made with hands. So not only is this trade of ours in danger of falling into disrepute, but also the temple of the great goddess Diana may be despised and her magnificence destroyed, whom all Asia and the world worship."*
>
> – ACTS 19:26-27 (NKJV)

Obviously, the kingdom of Satan was angry, as dark angels set their sight on disrupting Paul's influence by destroying his reputation. Nero sentenced Paul to death in Rome. When Paul knew that he would soon suffer beheading because of a lie, he wrote his final epistle to his spiritual son, Timothy. Look at these sad words:

> *"At my first answer no man stood with me, but all men forsook me: I pray God that it may not be laid to their charge."*
>
> – 2 TIMOTHY 4:16

> *"This you know, that all those in Asia have turned away from me, among whom are Phygellus and Hermogenes."*
>
> – 2 TIMOTHY 1:15

"Notwithstanding the Lord stood with me and strengthened me; that by me the preaching might be fully known, and that all the Gentiles might hear: and I was delivered out of the mouth of the lion."

— 2 TIMOTHY 4:17

Scholars estimate that Paul spent twenty years as a missionary traveling throughout Asia. He established several churches in Asia and at least three in Europe, including the church at Corinth, Greece. Yet, in his later years, because of Nero's lie, many Christians believed Paul was guilty of the fires in Rome. They believed the lies of a demonically controlled emperor, instead of vetting the information through Roman Christians.

CONSIDER THE SOURCE

A minister once shared with me that he had received a phone call from a man who was intent on telling him several horrible stories he had been told during a gathering of several people. The minister cut off the conversation and replied, "Wait a minute! You're believing what this person said? They're some of the biggest troublemakers and church hoppers I've ever see. They've lied on people before. You should consider the source."

Reputations precede people. Consider the source.

Those who desire to see others harmed will believe anything that undergirds their opinion. Those who give someone the benefit of the doubt will go to the one being accused and meet face-to-face to talk about it. If you want to help someone, you will challenge the person who is gossiping and backbiting. The right thing is to say, "I have no desire to listen to reckless gossip."

Christ's greatest opposition came from religious people who had their own beliefs and agendas and were threatened by His crowds, miracles, and bold teaching. Today, if a New Testament Sadducee taught that there is no resurrection, would you be surprised? The Sadducees were a religious sect in Christ's time who were considered the elite in Jerusalem. They denied the existence of spirits, including the human spirit, so they also denied the possibility of a bodily resurrection. A person's reaction to discourse on the possibility or impossibility of a future resurrection depends on the theories the listener heard and believed in the past. A past source of unbelief can continue to plant seeds of unbelief.

If a New Testament Pharisee taught a class on fasting, the first step might be to present a study from Isaiah 53:3-6 to explain the purpose of a fast. The fasts of Daniel in Babylon or Esther in Persia might be discussed. A good Pharisee would teach the importance of fasting twice a week (Luke 18:12), setting aside each Tuesday and Thursday as fasting days.

The Bible encourages fasting, but it does not tell you which days of the week to fast or how long to fast. The Pharisees had formed "traditions of the elders," which established extra-biblical rules, such as the exact days each week to fast. This religious sect always mixed truth with their own ideas that became traditions.

Within the Christian community, there are opposing theological views on several things. Consider water baptism. Some baptize in the name of Jesus, and others in the name of the Father, Son, and Holy Spirit. Most immerse, but some sprinkle. Is sanctification a one-time impartation, or is it progressive as a person continues to follow Christ and grow in their faith? Are the nine spiritual gifts in 1 Corinthians 12:7-10 still operational today, or did they cease with the apostles?

Every denomination has their doctrinal beliefs, and when I hear a specific doctrine taught, I usually know the denominational source of the teaching. Likewise, your information and the things you believe have an original source. That source could be the Bible, books, or something read on the internet. The source is important, whether it's the original source or second and third hand stories.

Events over the past several years have clearly demonstrated that, if the original source is incorrect, and if the original information is tainted or purposely weaponized, then the narratives being presented cannot be trusted. We have seen numerous news narratives and reports that have been labeled fake news, and different groups argue over the label. Once reports are investigated, we learn that people with a personal vendetta against someone else created the false narratives with the intent to harm those who disagreed with them politically. We have seen this tactic coming from people in Washington, D.C. for years and even decades.

Never take on the role of a fake news reporter. If the information proves to be false and defames the person's character, you could find yourself in the same position as the minister at the beginning of this chapter. Or you could face embarrassment as people label you an untruthful person who cannot be trusted.

CONSIDER THE INTENT

What is the intent or motivation of someone who creates, promotes, and shares false narratives? It should be clear that, if the purveyor of false narratives has a personal offense, hatred, or anger toward the person they are targeting, then one must consider that their motivation and intent are impure. If someone is earning money off the false narrative, it should cause you to question their motivation and intent.

A man once told me how an angry individual came to him to share some negative stories about an organization's leaders. After sharing the information, the angry man commented, "We're not trying to keep this quiet, so tell as many people as you want." Upon hearing this, the man knew something was not right. When a purveyor of negative information wants as many people as possible to know what he said, the listener must question their motivation and intent.

There is a reason why the verbal attacks against Christ never worked. For forty-two months, the Sadducees and Pharisees tried to divide Christ's ministry team and run off the outdoor crowds, but they failed. The cries of, "He is a blasphemer! He works miracles by the power of the devil!" had little to no impact because the people could see with their own eyes that the religious zealots were lying. If Christ's miracles were coming from satanic power, then why were the people always glorifying God? Why did Jesus always boast about the Father God before the multitudes?

If Satan had been the source, shouldn't Jesus have told people to lift up their hands and give Satan glory? A spiritual "blasphemer" would be *cursing* God; not *blessing* God. As one person said about Christ, "No man can do these miracles unless God is with him" (John 3:2). The fruit of Christ's ministry was the proof of His walk with God. *Fruit is the proof.*

A COMMUNIST SETUP

Years ago, a Romanian minister visited me and shared one of the saddest stories I had ever heard. When Romania was under a Communist dictatorship, there was a beloved pastor who successfully smuggled Bibles into the country. The Communist leaders believed he was the source, but they were unaware of how he accomplished this task.

To stop him, the communists selected a woman who was connected to the secret police, assigning her to infiltrate the church. Months later, after ingratiating herself into the congregation, this woman began to accuse the pastor of sexual immorality. With no evidence, the elders banned him from the ministry. He denied the accusations, but a few bullheaded elders refused to listen.

The former minister was an old man when communism finally collapsed in Romania. The communist plot was made public after someone obtained the case files from the former communist party headquarters. They discovered the original plans with detailed information about how they would take down the minister, the woman they selected, and an update on their success. The file was shown to church leaders. They brought the older minster into a ministers' meeting and repented to him with weeping.

Thankfully, his reputation was restored before he died. But only God knows how many people in a communist country were never reached with the gospel because this minister could no longer smuggle Bibles into the country.

It's puzzling how gullible so many Christians are to this kind of report. This minister had a track record in Romania and the church knew him well. Yet they believed the lies of a heathen communist infiltrator over a man of God.

Having been the object of a few newspaper articles over my lifetime, it is often what was *left out* that was most important. In one case, a woman on the inside of a newspaper contacted my wife to tell us the name of the man who was providing information to a reporter. We also learned that the writer of the article admitted that he hoped to break a story that would get national attention so he could be hired for a better job with a larger newspaper. Instead, he eventually was removed from the paper.

I have taught for years that I will pray for people, but I refuse to be pulled into another person's offenses. If I didn't start the war, if I'm not part of the war, then there's no reason for me to volunteer as a soldier and participate in someone's else's offense.

If you allow yourself to be pulled into this kind of thing, it will cause you problems in the future that you'll be sorry you brought upon yourself. It's better to put your mouth in neutral and say nothing, than to open your mouth and bring conviction or embarrassment upon yourself. You will never need to apologize for something you never said, nor will you have to answer to God for idle words you never spoke (Matt. 12:36). It's best to say, "Not interested" and change the subject. If the person persists, you might have to avoid them. *A cold shoulder is better than a hot mouth.*

People also have a problem with selective hearing, even when they're listening to a message in church. Studies show that people retain as little as twenty percent of what they hear. This is because they're listening while distracted, while thinking about how they're going to respond, or while making assumptions about the information they're hearing. This results in people hearing things they wanted to hear and filtering out things they don't want to hear. Selective hearing often causes problems.

The book of James sums up lessons to learn:

> *"Even so the tongue is a little member and boasts great things. See how great a forest a little fire kindles! And the tongue is a fire, a world of iniquity. The tongue is so set among our members that it defiles the whole body, and sets on fire the course of nature; and it is set on fire by hell.*

> *"For every kind of beast and bird, of reptile and creature of the sea, is tamed and has been tamed by mankind. But no man can tame the tongue. It is an unruly evil, full of deadly poison. With it we bless our God and Father, and with it we curse men, who have been made in the similitude of God. Out of the same mouth proceed blessing and cursing. My brethren, these things ought not to be so."*

> – James 3:5-10 (NKJV)

When confronted with questionable information and rumors, remember that an accusation is not evidence, and a rumor might not contain a shred of truth. If you repeat a story without firsthand verification and later learn that it was false, you have helped spread a lie. That is a serious transgression that can impact more than a person's reputation. Libel and slander can be subject to legal action and could become a costly payday for the person engaging in it. The person with whom the story originated may have a personal vendetta against someone and desire to harm that person or group of people. Consider that before you help them along.

You also break the commandment of not bearing false witness (Exodus 20:16). Never position yourself on the side of Satan. His plan is to accuse the brethren day and night (Rev. 12:10). Never make God's enemies your friends, and never make God's friends your enemies. A weaponized rumor can do just that.

CHAPTER 18

THREE WEAPONS MOST CHRISTIANS DON'T USE

The Christian's warfare arsenal is packed with weapons that can be used to battle mental, emotional, physical, and spiritual conflicts. In many cases, Christian soldiers conceal their weapons in storage in the event of a sudden war emergency, instead of wearing their armor continually (Eph. 6:12-18). Over decades of ministry, I have learned there are three spiritual weapons of war that are neglected by many believers. I have had to use all three of these in personal conflicts.

1. The Weapon of Silence

We have been instructed to use our mouth and words of authority to resist, rebuke, bind, and loose during all forms of spiritual struggles. Indeed, this is a leading principle of all conflict. Yet, how many know that sometimes we should *say nothing*?

The power of silence is a warfare weapon. Ecclesiastes 3:7 tells us there is a time to *speak* and a time to *refrain* from speaking. There is also a time to *stand up* and a time to *walk away*. Some people would be alive today if they had remained silent and turned their back on an aggressive person's rage.

The principle of silence was evident with Christ prior to His cru-cifixion. Christ knew that His death and resurrection would initiate the utter defeat of Satan's sin and death stronghold over mankind. Christ said, "Now shall the prince of this world (Satan) be cast out" (John 12:31), meaning cast out of his position of authority to control and dominate humanity. Christ later added, "The prince of this world is judged" (John 16:11), meaning that Christ's atoning work places an eternal sentence of doom on Satan's future, imprisoning him in the underworld abyss and eventually the lake of fire (Rev. 20:3).

A third verse revealed how Christ would handle His arrest, impris-onment, scourging, and eventual execution by crucifixion. He said, *"Hereafter I will not talk much with you. For the prince of this world is coming and has nothing in me"* (John 14:30).

Why would Christ refrain from talking with His disciples and not take time to explain in detail what was soon to occur? There were two possible reasons. First, Paul wrote that none of the rulers of this age knew God's purpose behind Christ's sufferings and His death, for had they known, they would not have crucified the Lord of Glory (1 Cor. 2:8). The more Christ talked and revealed His redemption plan, the more information Satan would have acquired, giving him the ammu-nition to attempt to stop the crucifixion, since he knew his defeat was imminent.

A second reason may have been a revelation an angel gave Christ when He was agonizing in the Garden of Gethsemane. During His arrest, Christ revealed that He was given authority to call twelve legions of angels to stop the whole process. Christ could have inserted His will above God's will and said, "I refuse to go through with this," thus demanding twelve legions—an estimated seventy-two-thousand angels—to release Him from death and take Him back to the Father in heaven.

There is an old war expression, "loose lips sink ships." In World War I and II, when soldiers sent letters home, they were instructed not to tell their families exactly where they were or what battle assignments were being planned, as the enemy could intercept the information and jeopardize the strategy.

Christ derailed any attempt of the adversary to keep Him from His assignment, simply by using *silence*. As He stood before high level religious and political leaders, including the High Priest Caiaphas (Matt. 26:3), Herod (Luke 23:8), and Pilate (Matt. 27:2), each man attempted to question Him about who He was or if He was the Son of God. The Bible says, "He answered them nothing" (Luke 23:9). His reaction was predicted 2,500 years ago when Isaiah, who wrote about the suffering Messiah said:

> *"He was oppressed, and he was afflicted, yet he opened not his mouth: he is brought as a lamb to the slaughter, and as a sheep before her shearers is dumb, so he opened not his mouth."*
>
> – ISAIAH 53:7

WHEN GOD SAYS BE SILENT

During an extended battle, the Lord gave me one of the most difficult instructions I had ever received. I was encountering relentless attacks from different directions at once, including from a few lying and demonically inspired people who were using my name to attract viewers to their social media platforms. One night at two o'clock in the morning I went to our International School of the Word facility to pray for a few hours. After three hours, I heard the Lord say to me, "Just keep quiet. Stay silent. Don't answer your adversaries or engage them in conversation. You must turn everything over to me and trust me, but don't respond to anyone who is attacking."

This was perhaps the most difficult instruction to follow that I have ever received. Months turned into years. During this time, various people came privately to my wife or me to expose things they had seen and heard, including what had led to part of the conflict. Then, unbeknownst to me, a trained expert began to investigate and expose several individuals.

You will learn, if you haven't already, that people think they can lie or stretch the truth to fit their own narrative, but even a half-lie is still a lie. It was shocking to hear the things we discovered being repeated, and it was very tempting to want to talk about it and expose things. But I tried to obey the word from the Lord, and eventually God came through.

During this challenging time, I realized that Satan does his work in *public,* so he can draw attention, generate chaos, confusion and gossip, and inflict maximum damage. But God does His best work in *silence,* often *behind the scenes.* Sometimes you feel that God is not working because you cannot see the results as fast as you desire. However, when He completes His work, everything can turn around in one hour.

When Job was grieving the death of his ten children, the loss of his livelihood, and his deteriorating health, he sought God for intervention while sitting in the dust and using pieces of pottery to pick the boils covering his body. He wrote:

> *"Behold, I go forward, but he is not there; and backward, but I cannot perceive him: On the left hand, where he doth work, but I cannot behold him: he hideth himself on the right hand, that I cannot see him: But he knoweth the way that I take: when he hath tried me, I shall come forth as gold."*
>
> – Job 23:8-10 (KJV)

In the Bible, the right hand of God represents His power and favor. The left hand of God represents His judgment or chastisement that permits tests and trials to come. Rabbis teach that God created light with His right hand and darkness with His left. The commandments that say "do this" will bring favor when we obey, while those that say "do not" will bring chastisement if they are broken.

What happens when God instructs us *not to use our mouth* during a crisis? Something happens when we remain quiet and still, and simply allow God to work:

> *"Be silent, O all flesh, before the* Lord: *for he is raised up out of his holy habitation."*
>
> – Zechariah 2:13 (KJV)

Amid your battle, understand that it is not always necessary to respond to critics or engage in verbal retaliation to defend yourself. That is like hitting a ball back and forth in a tennis match. When we are silent, we are telling the Lord that we are not in control of the battle, but He is. We choose not to throw more fire on an already red-hot conflict, but we are believing that God will rise from His holy habitation and become our weapon of war.

There is power in silence as you refrain from reacting to the attack or yielding to the devices of the enemy. Your silence demonstrates you will not be moved by your circumstances. Yes, there is a time to speak, but also a time to be quiet and claim this promise:

> *"No weapon formed against you shall prosper, and every tongue which rises against you in judgment You shall condemn. This is the heritage of the servants of the LORD, and their righteousness is from Me, says the LORD."*
>
> – Isaiah 54:17 (NKJV)

When you are silent, you also demonstrate to God that you have complete dependence upon Him. We dealt with a situation in which we learned that some actions taken against us were illegal, and discussions ensued that involved us taking legal action to deal with it. We ultimately chose to align our reaction with biblical instructions and let God handle it. The principle is that, if we desire God's favor, we must obey God's rules, including forgiving people because God forgave us (Matt. 6:12-15).

2. The Weapon of Trust

In the Old Testament, several Hebrew words are translated as *trust*. The meaning includes "to flee for protection; to confide in; to hope in; to place bold confidence in." In Hebrew and Greek, the word trust means "to be secure without fear."

It is our sense of fear and uncertainty that blocks our trust in the Lord. It is those "what ifs" that circulate in your mind. Common fears might be: What if the economy takes a hit? How will I pay bills? What if I get a terrible sickness? What if I lose my job? The truth is, *we often worry about situations that never transpire and fear the worst that never happens.*

When Job was at his lowest point, he made this statement, *"Though He slay me, yet will I trust him"* (Job 13:15). One of my favorite biblical promises is:

> *"Trust in the LORD with all your heart, and lean not on your own understanding; in all your ways acknowledge Him, and He shall direct your paths."*
>
> – PROVERBS 3:5-6 (NKJV)

Leaning on your own understanding means attempting to change an outcome using your own strength and abilities. You cannot strategize enough to overcome plots of the enemy by yourself and with your own understanding. Your enemies will sit around a table and plot plan A. If that doesn't work, then plan B will be set in motion. If that fails, they initiate plan C. This type of demonic conspiracy eventually will backfire on the instigator, as demonstrated in the Esther story, when Haman was hung on his own gallows.

My dear friend, Pastor Tony Scott, was asked a question by God one day: "Do you trust me?" Tony replied, "Yes, of course I do." Then the Lord told him "You have *intellectual* trust, but you don't *live* your trust."

In other words, God was telling Tony that he trusted in his mind, but his actions (or words) spoke to the contrary. This is double-mindedness and will hinder God's blessings in your life. James 1:6-8 warns that a double-minded person should not expect to receive anything from the Lord. We cannot operate in faith while also operating in unbelief. This is like a single fountain producing pure and bitter water at the same time.

Trust is a weapon because *your faith must rest in trust*. It is a foundation that your faith sits upon. A life of faith is grounded in trusting the truth and integrity of the Word, trusting the faithfulness of God, knowing that He will respond according to His Word and promises, and maintaining confidence in your prayers being answered. Hebrews 4:3 reveals, "For we who have believed enter that rest..."

Jesus slept in peace during a sudden violent storm on the Sea of Galilee. His boat was filling up with water. Yet He slept in peace (resting) because He had trust in His Father to protect Him because His hour (of suffering) had not yet come (John 2:4, 7:6, 30). Amid tests and trials, trust will bring rest to your soul and spirit.

When you are engaged in a trial that stretches your faith, you must consistently remain in prayer and thanksgiving. Do your best to rest in trusting the Lord without leaning on your own understanding or worrying about the outcome. Trust Him in all ways and He will direct your path.

3. The Weapon of God's Will

The third weapon is knowing that battles are won by operating in God's will. Every believer should desire to know and be positioned in the perfect will of God (Rom. 12:2). The *perfect* will of God is where He has *purposed* you to be. The will of God is not a one-time arrival point where we say, "I'm here and I have arrived," and then we live in years of bliss and perfection. God's divine purpose for us unfolds progressively, over time, as we move from level to level and assignment to assignment.

Year ago, the Lord told me to build a gathering place for a generation. By the time the building was finished, this gathering place was a 72,000 square foot, twenty-two-million-dollar facility.

During the building process, the whole country was experiencing an economic recession and none of the banks we worked with in Cleveland would give us a loan. We started building with four million dollars in our ministry account and would need another eighteen million dollars over the next two years to complete the facility. I had received two inspired words from the Lord before we began to build:

- He said build *Me* a gathering place, indicating the facility was *His* idea, not mine.

- He gave me the adage, "When it's God's *will*, it's God's *bill*."

I was to *direct* the project, but the Lord was to *pay* for the project. In two years, I never once doubted that God would provide the money for His plan. The Lord spoke, I knew His voice, and it gave me faith and confidence (trust) in His plan, purpose, and ability to pay. At the dedication of the 72,000 square foot facility, the Omega Center International building was paid in full.

The Apostle Paul followed the leading of the Spirit, yet he suffered many things for the sake of the Gospel. At his conversion, the Lord told him of "great things he must suffer for my name's sake" (Acts 9:16). A hindering spirit was assigned to Paul, yet he persisted unwaveringly, despite arrests, beatings, shipwrecks, stoning, and continual verbal abuse. God gave Paul a level of grace that was more than he needed to endure every level of conflict. *God never sends you any place without also giving you the grace and favor to bear up under the weight, burdens, and tests you will encounter.*

Being in God's will does not prevent you from experiencing battles, but it is a guarantee that God will be with you during all forms of conflict. He will never leave nor forsake you and is with you always (Matt. 28:20). *Being in God's will includes being in the right place with the right people at the right time.*

Things turn out for good when the Lord is with you (Rom. 8:28). Joseph was rejected by his brothers, sold as a slave, falsely accused of adultery, and sentenced to prison for nearly thirteen years. However, "the Lord was with him and whatever he did, the Lord made him prosper" (Gen. 39:3, 23). God's favor on Joseph was evident when God exalted him from the prison to the palace, placing him as second in charge under Pharaoh.

The Bible teaches that by faith and patience we inherit the promise. Hebrews 10:36 indicates, "For you have need of patience, that after you have done the will of God, you might receive the promise."

One of my wife's favorite statements is, "The devil will always overplay his hand." God will take advantage of any mistake the enemy makes. Pharaoh made a deadly error in judgment when he decided to chase the Hebrews and corner them at the edge of the Red Sea. God split the sea, held back the waters, made a path in the sea, and then caused the waters to crash around six hundred chariots. Pharaoh and his men were sent to a watery grave (Exod. 14).

When Satan inspired religious zealots to execute Stephen by stoning, God knew that was a mistake, because He was about to call into ministry the very man who directed the execution. His name was Saul of Tarsus, later known as the Apostle Paul (Acts 9).

When Paul was aboard a ship with two-hundred-seventy prisoners and caught in a deadly storm, Satan's intent was to drown Paul along with every other man on the ship. But God had other plans. The ship began to break apart near quicksand. All men on the ship came ashore on an island by floating on broken boards. The result was that, through Paul's ministry, the natives on the island converted to Christ. Paul later boarded a boat from that island that was the finest ship on the seas. He arrived at the port in Rome, where he remained two years, unhindered in the work of God (Acts 27-28).

On one occasion Paul and Silas were arrested, beaten, and confined in wooden stocks in a Roman prison. The mistake of the adversary was putting two Spirit-filled preachers in the same jail cell because, as it is written, "one can chase a thousand and two can defeat ten thousand" (Deut. 32:30). As the two worn out evangelists began singing a duet, the jail was shaken and the prisoners were loosed. This resulted in the head jailer and his family receiving salvation through Paul's preaching (Acts 16:25). The attacks of our adversary can turn into a mistake for him and a blessing for you!

When my son was addicted to drugs and alcohol, one night he ended up in the hospital emergency room and could have died. I told the adversary that he would pay for attacking my son. That was when I received a word from God to build the Omega Center building. We began to host an annual youth event that we call Warrior-Fest, which draws thousands of young people. Every time hundreds of young people pray a prayer of repentance or receive the baptism of the Holy Spirit, I consider this payback for the enemy making that one mistake of attempting to destroy my son.

Use your battles as fuel to inspire you to greater things in God. Remember, the enemy can initiate an unexpected battle at any moment. This is the *alpha* moment, the beginning of the war. However, it is impossible for Satan or any imp within his kingdom to know the outcome, or the *omega* (end) of your conflict.

Only Christ is the "alpha and omega, the beginning and the end" (Rev. 22:13). Alpha is the first and omega the last letter of the Greek alphabet. The letter omega represents the end or the conclusion of something. Satan initiated an alpha moment with Job. Within hours the enemy took everything that was precious to him. However, Satan could not control how the story ended. In Job 42, God blessed Job with double for his trouble (Job 42:10). Satan begins his attack (alpha), you remain faithful to trust God, then Jesus shows up in an omega moment and puts an end the trouble.

James wrote:

> *"Behold, we count them happy which endure. Ye have heard of the patience of Job, and have seen the end of the Lord; that the Lord is very pitiful, and of tender mercy."*
>
> – James 5:11

Long trials and tests require both faith and patience to inherit a positive outcome (Heb. 6:12). In my case, after a long conflict, including periods of ups and downs, my office manager walked in my office with a paper containing an official statement. It was an unexpected breakthrough revealing that a long conflict had suddenly ended. God had been faithful to end.

In summary, we need to use these three distinct weapons. The weapon of *silence* releases God to rise and fight your battle. The weapon of *trust* acknowledges that you know in your heart that all things will eventually work together for good because of God's Word and His promises. Then knowing and walking in the *will of God* means that you will prevail because you are in God's will. Christ used all three of these throughout His life and ministry, and so can we.

CHAPTER 19

SEVEN LIFE LESSONS ABOUT YOUR ADVERSARY

P aul wrote that we should not be ignorant of Satan's devices (2 Cor. 2:11). Since my teenaged years, I have read dozens of books and heard hundreds of messages on the topic of spiritual warfare. In the nearly half century that followed, I have had plenty of opportunity to use what I learned. Here are seven truths about warfare that believers should know.

1. Many of our battles are self-inflicted.

Years ago, I preached a message titled, "It's not the devil; it's you!" The point was to illustrate how many of our personal difficulties are not caused by the enemy or any of his spirits on assignment. They are simply the outcome of bad personal choices.

Look at the life of David. There is only one time when the Bible notes that Satan was directly involved with David, and that was when Satan stood up against Israel and provoked David to number Israel (1 Chron. 21:1). The Hebrew word for *provoke* means to incite, entice, persuade, stir up, and by implication, to seduce.

The Bible mentions certain failures in David's life. He committed adultery with a married woman that resulted in her becoming pregnant. Then he set up her husband Uriah to be killed in a frontline battle to cover the adultery. Although this was diabolical on many levels, not once does the Bible credit Satan with provoking David to do any of these things. David was motivated by his flesh nature caused by lust of the eyes. His character flaw eventually become his own trap.

When David exiled himself to a city named Ziklag to live among God's enemies, he made a reckless decision. Satan is not mentioned as having provoked David to do this. David made a poor decision that progressed from bad to worse.

How many times have we halted between two decisions; should I do this, or should I not? Sometimes we vacillate because our flesh pulls us toward one direction when we know we should choose the other. Thus, we open the door to a self-inflicted problem. It takes patience, time, and wisdom to resolve a self-invited crisis.

2. Most of Satan's victories occur because of our ignorance.

God noted that His people are destroyed for lack of knowledge (Hos. 4:6). Paul warned that Satan will take advantage of us if we are ignorant of his strategies (2 Cor. 2:11). The word ignorant is connected to the word *ignore.* To ignore is to disregard or refuse to pay attention to something, thereby causing a lack of informational awareness. Sometimes people hear without listening and paying attention; sometimes they see without comprehending or discerning.

It's one thing to be ignorant because the information is not available to you. It's another thing to have knowledge and understanding, but purposefully refuse to follow the right path. Ignorance is not bliss; it's dangerous. Being ignorant of Satan's strategies would be like taking an army to war without studying your opponent or having a battle plan. This is one reason why knowledge of the Bible is necessary. When Satan tempted Christ three times, Christ quoted three passages from Deuteronomy that countered Satan's offer. Satan flees when resisted (James 4:7). Spiritual knowledge is a primary weapon.

3. Demons love darkness, and darkness can become our mindset.

In Christ's day, one of His challenges was confronting the man-made traditions taught by the Pharisees. This religious sect taught errors such as, if you eat with unwashed hands, you could defile yourself and swallow an unclean spirit (Mark 7:2). If a person was healed on the Sabbath day, the Pharisees would accuse Christ of blasphemy, as it broke the rule of not working on the Sabbath. Pharisees were the professional rock throwers who looked for any opportunity to stone someone for breaking the rules, including their traditions of the elders.

When our mindset and thinking are wrong, we believe wrong things. When we believe wrong things, we make the Word of God of no affect (Mark 7). The Word of God brings light, and the absence of the Word brings darkness. Christ is the light, the Word is light, and this light opens the eyes, minds, and spirits of men and women.

The wrong mindset leads to deception. I have seen people influenced by darkness who initiated attacks and created confusion, then claimed that God told them to do it. Yet, God is never the author of confusion. Paul speaks of people whose understanding is darkened (Eph. 4:18). Only the Word and prayer can break wrong thinking and bring illumination, revelation, and inspiration.

4. Satan can resist your rebuke when you refuse to forgive others.

When a believer is operating in spiritual disobedience, especially regarding unforgiveness, Satan is not obligated to listen to you when you rebuke him or insist that he flee. Forgiving your enemies and those who despise you is not optional; it is not a mere suggestion from Christ for better success in life. In Matthew 6:14-15, Christ warned that, if you do not forgive others for their trespasses, neither will He forgive you. Unforgiving Christians can forsake their own mercy.

Christ also told His audience that if you are presenting an offering at the altar, but you remember that your brother has something against you, you should be reconciled to your brother, and then come and present your offering (Matt. 5:23-24). Unforgiveness will block your spiritual authority and weaken your resistance to the adversary. When abiding in bitterness and unforgiveness, your verbal rebuke becomes empty words. The words emerge from your lips, but not from the heart (Matt. 15:8). Forgiveness is mandatory to ensure victory in spiritual warfare.

5. Satan's plots can be planned years in advance.

Sometimes we are hit with a sudden attack that seems to come out of nowhere. It might seem as though the attack was just hatched a few days or hours ago. However, when the enemy makes his plans, he often establishes a plot years before the attack. He waits for the right time and uses his choice of people or organized groups to set his plots in motion.

At age thirty, Christ was baptized in water. Afterwards, He spent forty days being tested by Satan in the barren deserts of Judea. Satan assaulted Christ's identity, even challenging Him to prove that He really was the Son of God (Matt. 4:1-8). Forty-two months later, Satan recycled the same attack at the cross, challenging Jesus to prove that He really was the Son of God (Luke 23:37-39).

Notice the timing. Satan hit when Jesus was weak, hungry, and in great distress While He was fasting forty days, Satan suggested He turn rocks into bread (Luke 4:2-3). Forty-two months later, distressed and in intense pain after being beaten nearly to death and nailed to a cross, Jesus was challenged that, if He really was God's Son, He could rescue Himself from the cross.

I once experienced a strange battle that primarily involved a particular person. Months into the conflict, a man came to me and told me that this person admitted that "they had been planning to do this to you for several years." This is an example of strategies being planned years before they are enacted. Remember, your battle may have just manifested; however, the plot may have been hatched months or years ago.

6. You cannot defeat what you permit.

If you are personally convinced that a certain biblically defined sin is not really a sin, then you mentally set up a hedge to protect your own belief. At that point, no scripture, facts, or common-sense reasoning will change your mind. *Metanoeo*, the Greek word for repent, means to change your thoughts, attitudes, and behaviors so that they align with God's demands for right living. However, some people would rather *fight than switch.*

You will never change what you allow, and you will never receive help that you do not want. Sometimes a person will blame God for not stopping something bad that happened to them. Yet they persisted in the sin and danger, never allowing God to bring them freedom.

Time and again, once a person has been set free from sin and deception, they often shake their head and say, "How did I not see that? How did I let that happen? What was I thinking?" One woman said, "I was like Lazarus. I was bound up but didn't know it until I was set free!" That freedom can come only when you recognize you are a prisoner of your own mind or lusts, and you need and desire God's help.

7. God will chastise those whom He loves.

Scripture teaches that, those whom the Lord loves, He chastises (Heb. 12:6). The word *chastise* refers to discipline, as a parent would discipline an erring child. A parent might give warnings, but if the behavior doesn't change, the parent steps in to enforce the rules. The child dislikes the discipline, but it helps guide the erring child back to the right path.

God is our Heavenly Father, and we are His children. He understands that veering onto the wrong path is not only dangerous for us, but if not reversed, can eternally separate us from Him. God's chastisement is not done out of *spite* but out of *love*.

At times, the chastisement process might involve a personal crisis. Perhaps it will separate you from the wrong people or a situation that will cause you harm. A friendship separation might be challenging. However, when the Lord removes someone from your life, don't chase after them or pull them back into your life. The Lord removed them for a reason, and in the future you likely will understand why.

A chastisement is never pleasant, and it might continue until we finally learn our lesson. A few times in my life I experienced God's chastisement. Time passed and I assumed I had learned the lessons. But just as a child sometimes must be disciplined over and over before the message sticks, the same can be true with us.

Never despise the Heavenly Father's chastisement because the outcome is for your benefit. Paul told us the reason for a chastisement: "He (God) disciplines us for our good, that we may share in His holiness," and chastisement "yields the peaceable fruit of righteousness" (Heb. 12:10, 11). Many of us were disciplined growing up. In my case, I turned out fine—despite, or maybe because of—the discipline.

WHY DO SOME PEOPLE GET AWAY WITH EVIL?

Have you ever wondered why evildoers who slap on the Christian label never seem to be chastised by God? Why is it that strong Christians who are doing God's work experience discipline and chastisement, while those who do and say everything that contradicts Scripture get away with it? Why does God not discipline them, too?

I have watched belligerent, rebellious people who lack the fear of God attack decent people publicly in an almost obsessive manner. I have watched people who claim to be Christians follow these demonically inspired individuals and even repeat their lies. I asked God why He keeps allowing this, and I received a scripture that provided the answer:

> *"If you endure chastening, God deals with you as with sons; for what son is there whom a father does not chasten? But if you are without chastening, of which all have become partakers, then you are illegitimate and not sons."*
>
> — HEBREWS 12:7-8 (NKJV)

Those who receive spiritual correction from God are those whom He loves and calls His sons and daughters. The Holy Spirit spoke to me and said, "The reason you see people continually insult and attack with no chastisement is because those people are not My sons and daughters. They are illegitimate. They call me Lord, but I do not know them. They are participators with the workers of iniquity" (See Matt. 7:22-23).

We could compare some of these people to the deceived, self-righteous and hypocritical Pharisees who constantly nitpicked and tore down the ministry of Jesus with false accusations, lies, and slander. Yet, they pranced around in their tallit, with phylacteries protruding from their foreheads, declaring themselves the mouthpieces of God. All the while, Jesus called them a child of hell and said they would receive greater damnation in eternity (Matt. 23:14-15).

A true son or daughter of God should appreciate God's correction, as He is ensuring that you remove all spiritual and moral hindrances by His discipline. He is going to purify His bride. Those who are not disciplined are not of God, from God, or speaking for God. They could be reprobates whose punishment is set in eternity and not on earth. As such, all their idle words and carnal activity is still being recorded daily in the court of heaven, and their own words will condemn them before the great Judge of all men (Matt. 12:37).

SPIRITUAL WARFARE PRINCIPLES CONCEALED IN STORIES

During Christ's ministry, He encountered various natural storms on the Sea of Galilee. Each biblically recorded storm was designed to stop a specific assignment. The most significant storm occurred when Christ and His disciples were sailing to the other side of the lake and a great wind suddenly arose. This created violent and dangerous high waves that struck the boat and filled it with water (Luke 8:23).

This storm struck as Christ was sailing across the lake to deliver a man possessed with a legion of evil spirits. Eventually, Christ cast out the demons and permitted them to enter a herd of two thousand wild swine that were feeding on a nearby mountain. The swine ran violently down a steep bank and drowned in the sea (Mark 5:13).

The locals were familiar with this uncontrollable man. After he was delivered, the man proclaimed in Decapolis all the great things Jesus had done for him. When Jesus returned days later to minister in this same area, large crowds were so amazed, they gathered to hear Him and witness the miracles He performed. The testimony of the delivered man was heard in every city, creating interest in Christ's deliverance and healing ministry.

This one narrative illustrates an important point. The adversary will use any method—natural storms, wrong people, negative circumstances, or whatever means he can to hinder your progress or delay God's purposes. As fishermen, at times the disciples could avoid storms by keeping their boats tied and staying at port. Other times they were caught in the middle of a crosswind that required rowing head on into the rain and wind. Occasionally, Christ commanded the water to be at peace and the winds to cease (Mark 4:39).

There are times when we will discern the signs and sense a plot being hatched, and we can avoid it by using discretion and wisdom. There will also be seasons of trouble that hit so suddenly, there is no time to prepare. That requires patience and prayer to ride out the wind and waves until the storm concludes. At all times, we trust Christ to calm the situation with an infusion of His peace, just as He commanded the storm, "Peace, be still."

Spiritual knowledge is powerful, as we are not to be ignorant of the devil's strategies. In every type of battle, we can find scriptures to counter the attacks, and we can learn from the wisdom of others who have survived a similar struggle. Losing your battle is more of a *choice* than a *chance*. Winning the war is also a choice that you make when you come into agreement with God's wisdom and use His weapons of war.

CHAPTER 20

USING THE LAW OF REMEMBRANCE TO GAIN GOD'S FAVOR

After the Jews returned from seventy years of Babylonian captivity, Ezra and Nehemiah directed a massive cleanup and rebuilding of Jerusalem. The city walls, gates, and Temple lay in heaps of burnt wood and overturned stones. Nehemiah also began to spiritually clean house by demanding that the people, including Levites and priests, get their spiritual act together and return to the laws of God.

On several occasions, Nehemiah petitioned God to *remember him* (Neh. 13:14, 22, 29). He asked God to remember him for good and not to wipe out his good deeds. The Hebrew word remember is *zakar*, and it alludes to marking a specific event in time or recording information in an account. Nehemiah tapped into God's favor by using something I refer to as the "law of remembrance."

In Acts 10, the angel Gabriel appeared to an Italian centurion named Cornelius, a devout man who feared God, gave alms, and prayed continually. His steadfast prayers and financial contributions to the poor had been recorded in the court of heaven in a *Book of Remembrance*. God observed Cornelius' activities on earth and kept a written record of them. Acts 10:3-4 says that Cornelius experienced a vision of an angel calling his name and saying, "Your prayers and your alms have come up for a memorial before God" (Acts 10:4).

The phrase that stands out is *come up before God*. The imagery is that of righteous prayers being offered on the Golden Altar of Incense at the Temple in Jerusalem. David wrote, "Let my prayers be set before you as incense..." (Psa. 141:2). The Second Temple existed at the time of Peter, Paul, and Cornelius. Each morning and evening, a Levitical priest was selected to burn fragrant incense upon a golden altar (Exod. 40:26-27). The fire and incense produced "holy smoke" that rose to the ceiling of the Temple. The Jewish belief was that the words of the people's prayers were protected within the smoke as the prayers ascended upward and made their way into the Heavenly Temple. This was how prayers "went up" from earth to heaven.

After 150 days of water covering the earth during Noah's flood, God "remembered Noah" (Gen. 8:1). When four of the five cities at the southern end of the Dead Sea were consumed in fire, God remembered Abraham and sent Lot out (Gen. 19:29). The matriarch Rachel was unable to conceive children, yet God remembered Rachel and opened her womb (Gen. 30:22). After decades of living in Egypt, the Israelites cried out to God and He heard their groanings and remembered His covenant with Abraham, Isaac, and Jacob (Exodus 2:24). Hanna desired children but was barren. She wept and cried before the Lord, which captured God's attention. The Lord remembered her, blessing her with three sons and two daughters (1 Sam. 2:21). These examples reveal the power of God's "law of remembrance."

The idea of God remembering someone seems strange, since God is all present, all powerful, and all knowing. The idea of remembering something implies that you forgot before you remembered, such as losing your car keys, then suddenly remembering where you put them.

With Christ promising that He would be with us always, even unto the end of the age (Matt. 28:20), and that He would never leave us nor forsake us, why is it necessary for Him to remember us, when He cannot forget us?

THE HEAVENLY BOOK OF REMEMBRANCE

A *Book of Remembrance* is mentioned once in the Bible, in Malachi 3:16. Inscribed within the pages of this mysterious heavenly book are the names of those who are tithers and givers, those who fear the Lord, and those who witness to others. I believe this could be the same book referred to by the angel in Acts 10, where Cornelius is told that his prayers and offerings had come up as a memorial before God. The word memorial in Acts 10 has the same meaning as the word remembrance in Malachi 3:16.

When God remembered Noah, Hannah, Israel and others, He recalled what was recorded in the Book of Remembrance, just as He did with Cornelius, the first Gentile in Acts 10 to receive the New Covenant. When we pray, present our offerings and tithes, and walk in our redemptive covenant, our good deeds are recorded in this heavenly book. After our prayer and obedience, at the proper season in life, God recalls all that is written and releases His blessings and favor toward us.

Nehemiah was being challenged on several fronts. He dealt harshly with the disobedience of the priests and some of the people. He demanded strict observance to God's laws in the Torah. He knew that his stance would cause danger for him if a rebellion broke out against his authority. As he made decisions to stand with God, he asked God to remember him. We cannot be sure if Nehemiah knew about the Book of Remembrance, but God certainly did remember him. God allowed him to defeat three enemies from Samaria, all of whom were hindering the rebuilding project in Jerusalem. God protected Nehemiah, rebuked Satan's influence, and gave Nehemiah and Ezra favor to complete their restoration assignment.

LORD, REMEMBER ME

At a time when I experienced my greatest mental and physical battles, I lost both my strength and willpower to move forward. In the middle of the night, I drove to the T.L. Lowery building, which houses our online Bible school and global prayer center. I stood alone in the dark and called out to the Lord. I remembered the biblical story of the centurion whose servant needed to be healed. The town's people admired this Roman soldier and reminded Jesus that this man, a Gentile, loved the nation of Israel and had built the Jewish community a synagogue. In response to this and the centurion's great faith in Christ, Jesus healed the servant (Luke 7:1-10).

As I prayed, I began to remind God of things I had done for Him and His kingdom. I reminded Him that we had helped the poor and those in prison. I reminded him of the decades I had spent doing my best to fulfill His will. I said, "Lord, if this means something to you and your kingdom, remember me for the good."

During that time, I was too mentally and physically exhausted to deal with circumstances. However, throughout this test, I experienced several spiritual dreams where the Lord revealed people in the form of snakes, alligators, and piranhas. He showed me that the danger of each of these was their teeth and mouths. I would have a dream, and within days or weeks, whatever God showed me came to pass. The dreams exposed strategies being formed, who was behind them, and the eventual outcome. The Holy Spirit instructed me to ask for a mighty angel to assist me during this season. Over time, God intervened, often in unusual and unexpected ways, ultimately allowing His purposes and plans to prevail.

ASK GOD FOR HIS FAVOR DURING YOUR BATTLES

Decades ago, my dad was pastoring a church in Northern Virginia when he experienced a problem with three men who were being motivated by the enemy to hinder the church. During a service, Dad's head was bowed in prayer when he had a vision of an angel coming through the roof of the church and standing in the corner with a sword drawn over the congregation. The Holy Spirit revealed that the angel had come to deal with people problems in the church. Before long, the Lord allowed a somewhat violent incident to happen to one man that straightened him up, and the other two men suddenly moved out of state.

During the historic Brownsville revival, Pastor John Kilpatrick, worship leader Lindell Cooley, and evangelist Steve Hill were being assaulted every week by a local paper, whose editorial leader was behind hateful and misleading information that was purposed to shut down the mighty revival. Pastor Kilpatrick sought God for His Divine intervention. One day at a newspaper planning meeting, the young editor who headed up the conspiracy to destroy the revival suddenly fell over dead. Word spread at the newspaper that this was God's judgment.

My friend, Floyd Lawhon, pastored a church where a few belligerent members were hindering the ministry and God's work in the church. Lawhon went on a fast and asked God to remove the hindering people. The two ringleaders both died. Pastor Tony Scott has always said, "God judgment may be slow in coming, but it will eventually get there."

Rather than attempting to fight adversity using your own strength, clear your heart of all unforgiveness or bitterness, and petition God for

His assistance to intervene during your battle or conflict. You might not receive a breakthrough as quickly as you hope, as the Lord does use certain situations to prune our vine so that we will produce more fruit and learn to trust Him completely (John 15:2-26). You might feel as though you are standing alone with burning arrows being shot at you. This is when you must secure yourself behind your shield of faith and pray all manner of prayers in the Holy Spirit (Eph. 6:12-18).

God will remember you and consider all the times that you obediently helped the poor, fed the hungry, cared for widows and the fatherless, and assisted in spreading the good news of the Gospel. Eventually, God will either remove your enemies from your life, cause the attacks to fail, or give you the patience to endure, as He did with Paul (2 Cor. 12:9).

For a soldier of Christ who wears the armor of God, your adversaries will never win unless you give up and quit. *In due time, you will reap if you do not faint* (Gal. 6:9). God will remember you.

IN CONCLUSION

I hope that the insight in this book will help increase your knowledge, understanding, and wisdom as you continue your life's journey. It is important that we never exalt the influence and power of Satan and his demonic hordes, as Christ's death, resurrection, and the power of His blood and His name have defeated the enemy's authority over every believer.

At the same time, we cannot allow the enemy to take advantage of us, nor can we be ignorant of his schemes (2 Cor. 2:11). One of the most significant revelations for me was that many of the various attacks against me, my family, or the ministry have been set at cycles of twelve years. The twelve-year death pattern was also shocking.

One important point that the Holy Spirit wanted me to share with you in closing is that, if you begin to recognize a pattern in your family, do not live in fear or panic that something negative is about to occur in the future on that cycle. From my personal experience, to understand these seasons is to give you a heads up to begin fasting, praying, and claiming the promises in the Word of God in advance. Your advanced actions and prayers are a preemptive weapon that can change future circumstances and even restrain certain attacks.

When Hezekiah was told that he was going to die, he turned his face to the wall and began crying out to God, and the Lord added fifteen more years to his life (Isa. 38:5). Many times, Paul was near death. Yet God had assigned an angel to stand with him to ensure that Paul would live to fulfill his God-given assignments (Acts 27:23).

Each person reading this needs to be certain that you have experienced a redemptive covenant through the blood of Christ. The one and only way to break off the curse of the sins of the fathers and walk in newness of life is first to repent, turn from your sins, and allow Christ to make you a new creation. Make Christ both Savior and Lord of your life.

Christ has authority over the entire kingdom of Satan. However, we must close all doors that give access to a dark angel or any type of unclean spirit. Demonic spirits will often attempt to linger until they are exposed and cast out. Renounce any family sins, generational sins, or secret oaths, and confess the blood of Christ over your body, mind, and spirit and those within your household.

Mom
Susan
Kay
Kenneth
Chris—
Bob
Willie Mae
Papa Lee

Dad
Danny
Everret
Cathy
Bonnie

Aunt Lil
Uncle Bob
Alice
Papa Jim